MW00355565

 DOGFIGHT 1

Fw 190D-9
Defence of the Reich 1944–45

Robert Forsyth

OSPREY PUBLISHING
Bloomsbury Publishing Plc
Kemp House, Chawley Park, Cumnor Hill,
Oxford, OX2 9PH, UK
29 Earlsfort Terrace, Dublin 2, Ireland
1385 Broadway, 5th Floor, New York, NY 10018, USA
E-mail: info@ospreypublishing.com
www.ospreypublishing.com

OSPREY is a trademark of Osprey Publishing Ltd
First published in Great Britain in 2022
© Osprey Publishing Ltd, 2022

All rights reserved. No part of this publication may be
reproduced or transmitted in any form or by any means,
electronic or mechanical, including photocopying, recording,
or any information storage or retrieval system, without prior
permission in writing from the publishers.

A catalogue record for this book is available from the British
Library.

ISBN: PB 9781472849397; eBook 9781472849328;
ePDF 9781472849304; XML 9781472849311

22 23 24 25   10 9 8 7 6 5 4 3 2 1

Edited by Tony Holmes
Cover and battlescene artwork by Gareth Hector
Ribbon and technical diagrams by Tim Brown
Armament artwork by Jim Laurier
Maps by www.bounford.com
Index by Angela Hall
Typeset by PDQ Digital Media Solutions, Bungay, UK
Printed and bound in India by Replika Press Private Ltd

Osprey Publishing supports the
Woodland Trust, the UK's leading
woodland conservation charity.

MIX
Paper from
responsible sources
FSC® C016779

To find out more about our authors and books visit www.
ospreypublishing.com. Here you will find extracts, author
interviews, details of forthcoming events and the option to
sign up for our newsletter.

Previous Page: Fw 190D-9 Wk-Nr. 211934 of II./JG 6,
assigned to that Gruppe's Technical Officer, was photographed
at Fürth after being surrendered to American forces. Note the
supercharger intake on the right side of the cowling, and the
Junkers VS 111 wooden constant-speed hydraulic variable pitch
propeller. Also visible are the DF loop at rear and antennae for
the FuG 25a IFF and FuG 16ZY VHF transceiver. (EN Archive)

Front Cover Artwork: On 21 March 1945, a small formation
of Soviet Il-2 *Shturmovik* fighter-bombers carried out a low-level
attack on Prenzlau airfield in northeastern Germany. It was home
to IV./JG 3, whose *Stab* at least was, by this time, equipped with
Fw 190D-9 fighters. Moments before the attack had taken place,
however, the 'Alarmstart' was sounded over the airfield and a
number of the *Gruppe's* 'Doras' were able to get airborne just as
the Soviet attack commenced. The hurried Luftwaffe response
was led by the *Gruppenkommandeur*, Oberleutnant Oskar Romm,
a 91-victory ace who had been awarded the Knight's Cross on
29 February 1944. During the engagement fought overhead
Prenzlau airfield, Romm was able to shoot down one of the Il-2s
for his 92nd, and final, victory.

Acknowledgements – I would like to extend my thanks to Eddie
J. Creek, J. Richard Smith, Tony Holmes, Donald Caldwell,
Gerhard Kroll(+), Hans-Ekkehard Bob(+), Herbert Kaiser(+),
Walter Krupinski(+), Heinz Radlauer(+), Dr James H. Kitchens
III, Judy and Jerry Crandall, Nick Grant, Shaun Barrington,
Professor Patrick G. Eriksson, Geoff Nutkins, Dietmar Hermann
and Tomáš Poruba. Dietmar Hermann, Axel Urbanke, Jerry
Crandall and the triumvirate of Marc Deboeck, Eric Larger and
Tomáš Poruba have written exceptional works on the Fw 190D-9,
and their volumes have been at my side during the writing of
this book. As the reader will observe, this study is enriched by
several narrative accounts that I have borrowed gratefully from
the aforementioned authors, but most of all from the studies
by Donald Caldwell on *Jagdgeschwader* 26. His books contain
extraordinary levels of detail on Fw 190D-9 operations. I urge
those who wish to learn more about this intriguing aeroplane to
seek out the works by these authors.

Contents

CHAPTER 1
IN BATTLE

By 12 April 1945, as the shrinking Third Reich crumbled under the weight of Allied and Soviet armies advancing into it from the west and the east respectively, infantry and armoured units of Lt Gen Evelyn Barker's VIII Corps – a part of the British Second Army – had crossed the Weser river and had pressed onwards across the fields and heaths of northern Germany. As they advanced, the 1. *Fallschirm-Armee* (Parachute Army) fell back, establishing bridgeheads over the Aller river. Here, Barker's tanks, which had moved rapidly northeast to reach the town of Uelzen, were slowed. According to 21st Army Group commander, Field Marshal Bernard Montgomery, enemy resistance stiffened and there followed four days of 'hard fighting'.

Coordinating Luftwaffe air support for the beleaguered German ground forces fighting in the Uelzen area was the Luftwaffe's 14. *Fliegerdivision*, which had just taken over tactical control of *Stab*, I., II. and IV./JG 26. Since the autumn of 1944, these component *Gruppen* of the famous 'Schlageter' Geschwader had gradually replaced its Focke-Wulf Fw 190As with Fw 190D-9s, known colloquially as the 'long-nosed Dora' on account of its lengthened nose, which housed a 1,726hp Jumo 213A engine. There had been some degree of expectation for the long-awaited and much vaunted new fighter, and the limited numbers which had been delivered had proved generally satisfactory.

The aircraft was built as an aerial interceptor and air superiority fighter to deal with the twin threats of improved Allied fighter designs such as the British Tempest V and the American P-51B/D Mustang, as well as the prospective debut of the B-29 Superfortress bomber in the skies over Europe. Due to tactical exigencies, the D-9 had been deployed as a fighter, as an airfield protection aircraft and, increasingly, as a fighter-bomber.

On 12 April, however, the 14. *Fliegerdivision* would deploy the Fw 190D-9s of I./JG 26, commanded by Major Karl Borris and based at Stade, west of Hamburg, in their primary intended role. Conditions were good, with any early morning cloud dissipating to leave clear skies. Furthermore, in an increasingly rare occurrence, a delivery of aviation fuel had reached the airfield in sufficient quantity to mount several sorties.

At 1230 hrs, Oberleutnant Hans Dortenmann, the *Staffelkapitän* of 3./JG 26, took off to lead 12 'Doras' carrying drop tanks for maximum range, comprised of a *Schwarm* of four aircraft from each of the *Gruppe's* three *Staffeln*, on what would be his second operation of the day. He had already flown an early morning mission to strafe ground targets in the vicinity of the Weser, and had observed a mass of enemy vehicles around Bremen before being forced to return to base due to enemy antiaircraft fire. This second mission was intended as an armed reconnaissance of the lower Elbe river.

Just over 470km away, 12 Tempest Vs of the 2nd Tactical Air Force's No 33 Sqn took off from the Dutch airfield of Kluis on an offensive fighter sweep to the Uelzen area. The fighters were led aloft by the unit CO, Sqn Ldr A. W. Bower. No enemy aircraft were subsequently sighted once over Uelzen, so the RAF fighters split up into sections to attack ground targets on their way home. Leading Blue Section was South African Air Force pilot Capt E. D. Thompson, who continued to head eastward at 8,000ft with his Tempest Vs until around 19km northeast of Uelzen, when enemy motor transport was observed below through an increasingly hazy sky. The Tempest Vs descended and carried out three stafing runs, shooting up four vehicles and damaging a fifth. As Thompson pulled up from his third attack, he spotted what he thought were Bf 109s:

Karl Borris was the *Gruppenkommandeur* of I./JG 26 from 1 August 1944 through to war's end, but he spent the entire war flying with the *Geschwader*. His *Gruppe* received its first Fw 190D-9s in mid-December 1944. Borris, seen here with the rank of Hauptmann, had a reputation as a steadfast pilot and unit commander. He claimed a Spitfire flying the Fw 190D-9 on 14 January 1945 for his final victory, raising his personal score to 43, of which no fewer than 28 are listed as Spitfires from June 1940. (EN Archive)

> I did a 190° turn, and when at about 2,000ft I sighted 15+ Me 109s [sic] passing overhead at about 5,000ft, flying West to East. I reported that we were being bounced, and dropped tanks.

Indeed, at that very moment, Dortenmann's formation spotted the Tempest Vs, and a wild, turning dogfight began north of Uelzen, with aircraft weaving from 800m down to ground level. Leutnant Karl-Heinz Ossenkop was flying an Fw 190D-9 in the 2. *Staffel Schwarm* led by *Staffelkapitän* Leutnant Waldemar Söffing. He recalled (Caldwell, *JG 26 War Diary*, pg 463):

> Eight Tempests were crossing beneath us. We dropped our tanks and dived to the attack. They fired their rockets into the empty sky. A turning combat began. I reached firing position on my target; because of my superior height, I needed little lead. At 100–70m distance I gave him a short salvo. The Tempest burst into flames, and seconds later, crashed to the ground. The pilot had no chance to get out. I saw several parachutes and smoke plumes, and heard several victory cries over the radio.

Clad in late-war leather flying gear, Leutnant Waldemar Söffing (centre), *Staffelkapitän* of 2./JG 26, is flanked by Leutnant Karl-Heinz Ossenkop (left) and Oberleutnant Georg Kittelmann (right) at Fürstenau in February 1945. Flying a D-9, Söffing would claim a Tempest V of No 33 Sqn shot down over Uelzen on 12 April for his 28th of an eventual 34 victories, while Ossenkop also claimed one of the RAF fighters that same day for his second victory. Kittelmann was shot down and killed near Troisdorf by a P-47 while flying a 'Dora' on 25 February 1945. (Dietmar Hermann Collection)

For the Tempest V pilots bounced by the Fw 190D-9s, it was a tough struggle to recover the ascendency in the engagement, as Thompson later reported (still mistaking the Focke-Wulfs for Messerschmitts):

I saw two Me 109s [sic] coming down on my No. 2, so I broke round hard to port, endeavouring to cover him, when I sighted 2 Me 109s coming down on my tail and was forced to break round hard to starboard. I saw Blue 3 coming up to cover Blue 2. At this moment I lost sight of Blue 2 while taking evasive action. By this time most of the Me 109s had joined in the fight, and it was almost impossible to keep track of the whole of my section. During this time, my height had varied from 0ft to 3,000ft. While at about 1,000ft, one Me 109 came down on my port side and pulled away from me, exposing himself to an easy attack. I opened fire from about 200 yards and saw him go diving straight into a wood and blow up in flames. Almost immediately I found myself being attacked from behind at very close range.

Thompson's assailant was most probably Leutnant Söffing, who had latched onto his fighter and fired a burst at it. As the No 33 Sqn pilot described:

I received severe damage to my port aileron, so broke down hard to ground level, endeavouring to break off the engagement, but this Me 109 maintained his chase and I found I was only able to evade his fire by violent weaving as near to the ground as possible.

As Karl-Heinz Ossenkop recounted (Caldwell, *JG 26 War Diary*, pg 463):

I next saw Söffing chasing an escaping Tempest at ground level. 'Come with me! We'll catch him!' he shouted. I flew left, Waldemar flew right, but the Tempest pulled away from us at tree-top height, despite our use of full throttle and MW 50 methanol injection.

At least one other No 33 Sqn pilot, South African Flg Off D. J. ter Beek, reported having to dive away to escape the scene, weaving, at ground level, under attack from several Fw 190D-9s. It was only when he reached the bombline that the Focke-Wulfs broke away.

The JG 26 pilots claimed five victories and one probable, for the loss of Leutnant Erich Asmus of the *Gruppenstab* who most likely fell to Thompson's guns. No 33 Sqn had actually lost two aircraft and their pilots, with Flt Sgts P. W. C. Watton and J. Staines being posted as missing. The latter was on only his second operational flight, having joined the squadron just ten days earlier. It is likely that one of these pilots was Leutnant Ossenkop's first claim.

Söffing's attack on Thompson's Tempest V had shot away the outboard half of its port aileron and left the main wing holed. The South African managed to fly his aircraft back to Kluis, where he made a flapless landing, touching down at about 130mph and narrowly avoiding nosing up into the sand at the end of the runway.

This brief but fierce engagement was one of several that took place over northern and central Germany during the last weeks of the war between what were two of the finest piston-engined fighters of the conflict. Despite being outnumbered and usually lacking the training of their Allied counterparts, it demonstrates how pilots flying the Fw 190D-9 could compete with, and defeat, one of the best Allied fighters in aerial combat.

That evening, it was the turn of the D-9s from II./JG 26 to conduct one of their now regular missions to strike at enemy artillery positions and supply dumps around Bremen using 250 or 500kg high-explosive bombs, or AB 250 or SC 250 containers loaded with 2kg SD-2 *Splitterbombe* (fragmentation) bomblets. The AB 250 was not a popular ordnance choice amongst 'Dora' pilots since the ability to jettison containers was not always reliable and the impact fuses of the bombs could not be disarmed after take-off.

For several days in April 1945, II./JG 26's D-9s carried out such low-level fighter-bomber missions. Typical was the one flown on 17 April, when 14. *Fliegerdivsion* despatched no fewer than 47 Focke-Wulfs to attack enemy motor transport columns in the Soltau–Uelzen–Salzwedel area. Pilots claimed two Tempest Vs shot down and a third one probably destroyed during the mission (in fact just one Tempest V was lost), with three D-9s lost and a fourth damaged in return.

Despite their paucity in number, the 'Doras' of JG 26 remained a thorn in the side of Allied ground forces fighting in Lower Saxony through to VE Day, the appearance of the aircraft having raised the stakes for Allied fighter pilots operating in-theatre.

Erfurt-built Fw 190D-9 Wk-Nr. 500342 of II./JG 26 has its engine run up at Reinsehlen in December 1944. The *Gruppe* was undergoing conversion to the 'Dora' when this photograph was taken. The white '9' on the rudder is not a tactical code, but rather a temporary number used for ferry or delivery flights. (EN Archive)

CHAPTER 2

SETTING THE SCENE

In September 1944, the Luftwaffe fighter arm was at a pivotal and indeed perilous point in its existence, under pressure from a growing list of priorities, but compromised by shortcomings which it could not control. The Allied landings in Normandy in June had forced the *Oberkommando der Luftwaffe* (OKL – Luftwaffe High Command) to move nearly 1,000 fighters into France drawn from six *Geschwader*. But operating conditions on the 'Invasion Front' proved testing in the extreme.

Nevertheless, the *Jagdwaffe* fought a determined yet ultimately futile battle there, often from the most rudimentary emergency airfields, against an enemy significantly more powerful than itself and able to draw upon reserves and resources which it could not match. Major Hans-Ekkehard Bob commanded the Bf 109G-equipped II./JG 3, based at Evreux, and recalled the constant presence of enemy fighters:

> We were often attacked taking off, causing one aircraft taking off to be blocked by another. Our position was extremely unpleasant. We reckoned in operating strength we were outnumbered ten-to-one. In fact, operations were really more an exercise in self-preservation.

Likewise, Oberfeldwebel Herbert Kaiser, another experienced Bf 109G pilot, flew with 7./JG 1 and remembered:

> We had to take off in the smallest of flights (usually two to four aircraft) due to the Allied fighters, which almost always waited above our airfields for our fighters to emerge from cloud cover. We would be forced to sneak towards the target area by hedge-hopping over the terrain to take advantage of as much natural camouflage as possible. Flying just a few metres above the ground kept us off the radar screens, but sometimes put us into the side of a hill. We would only climb to altitude once we reached the point of attack. At this time the odds were against us, and you could

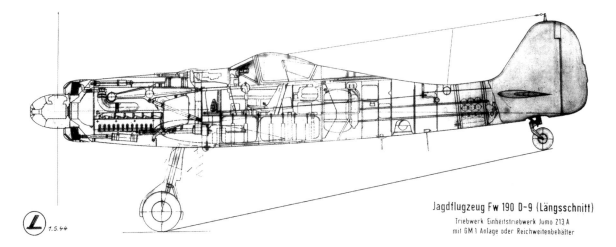

Jagdflugzeug Fw 190 D-9 (Längsschnitt)
Triebwerk Einheitstriebwerk Jumo 213 A
mit GM 1 Anlage oder Reichweitenbehälter

1.5.44

A Focke-Wulf drawing of the Fw 190D-9 dated 1 May 1944, showing the aircraft installed with a Jumo 213A engine and the GM 1 nitrous oxide injection boost system for higher-altitude performance. (EN Archive)

count on the fingers of one hand the days you expected to live. Frankly, I am amazed Luftwaffe fighter pilots had any nerve left at all, let alone the ability to attempt to fight under such conditions.

On one level, the *Jagdwaffe* had to fight back against, let alone repel, the enemy invasion forces that attacked and threatened its own airfields, but on another level it also had to render support to German ground forces as they began their retreat across northern France towards Belgium and the Netherlands, and ultimately, the frontier of the Reich itself. But as the former *General der Jagdflieger* (General of Fighters) Adolf Galland recorded after the war:

> It is characteristic of an air force that to a relatively small group at the front belongs a huge machinery at the rear. It is difficult enough to maintain aggressive strength when advancing, but in a retreat, the weight and bulk of these supporting services have a proportionately negative effect the quicker and more disorganised the retreat becomes.

During the late summer of 1944, the Allied tactical air forces applied increasing pressure on the German retreat across France, harassing airfields, logistics, railways and the signals infrastructure, as well as targeting general storage facilities and supplies of fuel – a commodity which suffered increasingly from shortages.

Furthermore, German fighter units had to maintain their defensive operations against the Allied strategic bombing offensive that continued to pound the Third Reich and the remaining occupied territories virtually every day. In this regard the Operations Staff of the OKL still saw the *Jagdwaffe*'s prime mission in September 1944 as one of air defence, and to ensure 'domination of the air over friendly territory and the destruction of enemy aircraft by day and night'. In reality, before 'domination' could be achieved, a more immediate goal was 'equality', and even on that count, the *Jagdwaffe* was substantially outgunned by the enemy's aerial capabilities.

The main threat came from improvements to the Allies' air superiority fighters. The American P-51D Mustang, which made its debut in northwest Europe in the early summer of 1944, was appearing in increasing numbers, equipping more groups. This superlative variant of the Mustang saw the internal fuel load of 269 gallons increase to 489 gallons by the fitment of two 110-gallon wing-mounted drop tanks. If handled well, the Mustang's Rolls-Royce Merlin engine could consume less than 60 gallons per hour while cruising at 260mph when flying escort missions. This gave it the 'legs' it needed to escort the Eighth Air Force's heavy bombers on deep penetration missions. By April 1944, 6,000 P-51Ds had been ordered.

Furthermore, British Spitfire IXs, XIVs and XVIs saw improvement to their basic configurations in the summer and autumn of 1944, including the installation of a gyro gunsight (although this was not popular with all pilots), the fitting of the 'E' Type wing with its refined armament, all-round vision bubble canopies and increased fuel loads. Thus, like the Mustang, the Spitfire had evolved into a true multi-role aircraft: an air superiority fighter, interceptor, long-range escort, fighter-bomber and reconnaissance aircraft.

In addition, USAAF radial-engined P-47 Thunderbolt and RAF/RCAF Typhoon fighter-bombers attacked German transport and airfields with cannon, bombs and rockets.

Compounding this daunting reality for the Luftwaffe was the fact that, generally, Allied pilots benefited from far more extensive and graduated training than did their German counterparts. Reductions in the fighter training programme as far back as the autumn of 1943 meant that replacement pilots were reaching operational units with an average of 148 hours on powered aircraft.

And it was not just enemy fighters that exposed the inadequacy of the training that new *jagdflieger* were receiving by late 1943. Poor weather conditions over western Europe often proved too much for novice pilots, as Reich Generalleutnant Josef Schmid, commander of

A wooden wind tunnel model of the planned Fw 190D-1, showing the earliest 'Langnase' design. Despite the hole in the spinner, it was not foreseen that this variant was to have an engine cannon. In any case, the D-1 and the follow-on D-2 were abandoned at an early stage and replaced by the D-9. (EN Archive)

I. *Jagdkorps* (which played a key role directing fighter defence over the Reich) noted somewhat obliquely in his report summarizing operations in January 1944:

> The technical deficiencies of German fighter aircraft and the low training standard of replacement fighter pilots precluded steadily successful and effective combat against American superiority at high-altitude. Thus, January 1944 was again characterised by the inability of German forces to provide an effective defence against American daylight attacks on the Reich, let alone prevent them. Only the utmost caution in employing aircraft in bad weather – especially when take-off and landing conditions were uncertain – was able to keep German losses within reasonable limits.

January saw the Luftwaffe lose 16.9 per cent of its fighter pilots. The situation had not improved by the summer, as Schmid explained:

> Heavy losses, as well as the great physical and psychological strain imposed on German fighter pilots, reduced the combat value of our units in April and May 1944. The young replacements showed deficiencies in flying and radio usage. They lacked combat experience, particularly in respect to high-altitude operations. Time and opportunities for training in the operational units was lacking to an increasing extent. The shortage of qualified formation leaders increased. The excessive strain caused by almost uninterrupted commitment resulted in combat fatigue. Experienced fighter pilots reached the limit of their efficiency. They were worn out by the many missions they had flown and needed a rest. All these factors resulted in a number of failed missions.

Over the coming months, the result of this situation was that, inevitably, losses climbed still further. Yet, for the time being at least, the Eastern Front held firm along the Vistula river – that in itself was a line which showed just how far German forces had retreated in the East since the summer of 1943. It was questionable just how long the Luftwaffe would be able to maintain an effective defensive stance on the Western Front, above the Reich, in the East and in Italy.

Nevertheless, September 1944 did see record deliveries of more than 3,000 new or repaired single-engined fighters, largely as a result of the efforts of the *Jägerstab* – a committee of aircraft industry chiefs and production specialists set up by Albert Speer and Erhard Milch in March. It was their job to oversee and coordinate the output of the German fighter production industry.

Within this quantity were the first examples of a new, greatly anticipated, high-speed, high-altitude, piston-engined fighter from Focke-Wulf – the Fw 190D-9. Given the aforementioned scenario, its appearance was timely and welcome, for not only did the *Jagdwaffe's* Bf 109s and Fw 190As have to deal with the P-51, P-47, Spitfire and Typhoon, yet another superb medium- and low-level British fighter was about to make its debut in September in the form of the Hawker Tempest V, adding to the pressure on the Luftwaffe's squadrons.

Prof. Dr. Dipl.-Ing. Kurt Tank, a superlative aircraft designer, sitting in the cockpit of an Fw 190 – perhaps the design he is best known for. Tank saw the D-9 as an 'interim solution' to the shortcomings of the earlier radial-engined variants of the Fw 190 which had required continual revision ahead of the introduction of the Ta 152. (EN Archive)

At the core of the development of the Fw 190D-9 was the need to fit a new type of engine into the Fw 190 airframe to replace the existing BMW 801 radial. Prof. Dr. Dipl.-Ing. Kurt Tank, Focke-Wulf's chief designer, was mindful of the fact that the performance of the BMW fell away at altitude, and as early as 1941 he had considered a suitable replacement which would give the Fw 190 the edge over the Spitfire. Circumstances largely dictated the events that followed, as Tank described:

Hardly was the Fw 190 flying at the beginning of the war before it had to be extensively redesigned, enlarged and made more powerful still. In no time at all, the requirements of very many pieces of auxiliary equipment connected with the armament and communications of the aeroplane forced up its weight, and at the same time new and more powerful engines were becoming available.

The solution to Tank's search lay in the Junkers Jumo 213, and an example of the inverted V12 engine was installed in modified Fw 190A airframe Wk-Nr. 0039 CF+OX, which became the V17 prototype and the first of five test aircraft planned under this configuration. Ground trials proceeded in conjunction with similar tests using a Daimler-Benz DB 603 engine. Although delays in delivery meant that Junkers was not in a position to supply Focke-Wulf with the first Jumo 213 until the end of July 1942, the engine had the edge over the DB 603 as a result of its pressurised cooling system. With high boost settings, the Jumo 213 could produce 1,750hp at 3,250rpm, giving the performance that the Fw 190 needed.

The V17, which was installed with an annular radiator, flew for the first time on 26 September 1942 from Focke-Wulf's works at Hannover-Langenhagen. Generally, things went well. The V17 was distinctive because of its longer nose – a feature necessary to accommodate the heavier Jumo engine, which was some 60cm longer than the BMW 801. This additional length duly meant ballast needed to be added aft of the V17's cockpit in order to prevent any destabilising issues with the centre of gravity –

The Jumo 213A-0 as seen in a service document dated June 1942. Much was expected of this engine for the Fw 190D-9, but as with other German powerplants of the period, it arrived late and in insufficient quantities. A development of the Jumo 211, the engine employed a pressurised cooling system, a strengthened crankshaft and an engine block with smaller external dimensions, but retained the former's bore and stroke. With the addition of higher boost settings, the Jumo 213A-0 was designed to produce 1,750hp. (EN Archive)

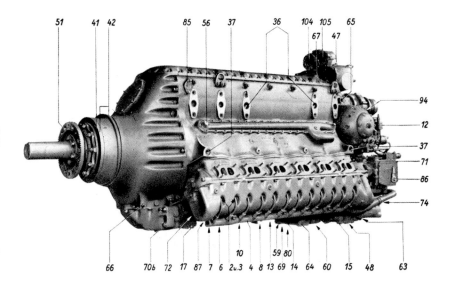

The Fw 190 V17 Wk-Nr. 0039, photographed at Langenhagen in late 1942, was powered by a Jumo 213 engine. It is seen here undergoing an engine test run and has an enlarged tail fin and rudder. The V17 would eventually become the third D-9 prototype. (EN Archive)

130kg of lead plating in the radio compartment, 12kg in the vertical tail fin and 15kg in the jacking tube. Later, as a much more elegant solution to countering the forward weight, the rear fuselage was lengthened by 500mm.

The aircraft was redesignated the V17/U1, and it became the first true *'Langnase'* ('long nose') prototype. Focke-Wulf test pilot Bernhard Märschel found that when the aircraft was powered by a Jumo 213A-2 there was a great improvement in its performance at altitude over the BMW 801D. Furthermore, in a dive, the D-9, with its reduced drag from a narrower radiator profile, was faster than the earlier Fw 190 with its wider radial engine and cowling.

From July 1943 to April 1944, testing continued using Jumo 213s in five prototype machines, the V17, the V19–V21 and the V25. In a Focke-Wulf overview of late February 1944, it was stated that:

> The Fw 190D single-seater is the result of a requirement to install the Jumo 213A in the Fw 190A-8 airframe with the minimum possible modifications to the fuselage. It is intended that the Jumo 213A standard powerplant should find the widest possible use. The Fw 190D-9 represents an interim solution pending the introduction of the Ta 152, and it will be delivered in limited numbers.

Based on a standard Fw 190A-8 airframe, the Fw 190 V53 Wk-Nr.170003 DU+JC, seen here at Langenhagen in June 1944, was fitted with a Jumo 213C engine that would allow installation of a centreline cannon. The aircraft was test-flown rigorously in the summer of 1944 to assess climb performance, airspeed, instruments, coolants, control forces, flight characteristics, hydraulics and temperatures. (EN Archive)

Hauptmann Robert Weiss, *Gruppenkommandeur* of III./JG 54, photographed in France in 1944. His *Gruppe* would be the first to fly the Fw 190D-9 on operations. On 28 September 1944, Weiss shot down a Spitfire PR XI of No 541 Sqn while flying a D-9, and in doing so claimed the first aerial victory for the 'Dora'. (EN Archive)

In June and July 1944, early Fw 190A-8s Wk-Nr. 170003 and Wk-Nr. 174024 were reconfigured under the suffix D-9 (the 'D' became referred to as 'Dora') at the Focke-Wulf plant at Adelheide. Assigned the prototype numbers V53 and V54, respectively, the former was fitted with a Jumo 213C that was capable of carrying a centreline cannon firing through an opening for a blast tube in the propeller hub – a *Motorkanone*. A weapon in this location had the advantage of being mounted along the pilot's line of sight, and it also created less drag than a gondola-mounted cannon, thus having less of an impact on speed and manoeuvrability. Conversely, the recoil of the centrally-mounted weapon when it was fired could have an impact on the engine, leading to mechanical problems and possible damage.

The main task of the V54 was to trial the MW 50 methanol-water power-boosting system, which was based on a solution of 50 per cent methanol, 49.5 per cent water and 0.5 per cent anti-corrosive fluid. The solution was injected directly into the supercharger for limited periods not exceeding ten minutes. In aerial combat, the boost increased the power of a Jumo 213 engine by at least 300hp to 2,000hp for short periods. Such a system came with the added benefit of needing only the installation of purpose-made spark plugs to modify the engine. However, its one side-effect was that the corrosive nature of methanol eventually reduced engine life.

The first production machines rolled out of Focke-Wulf's Sorau factory towards the end of August 1944 and were delivered, following assessment and acceptance by the Luftwaffe's *Erprobungsstelle* at Rechlin, to III./JG 54, under the command of Hauptmann Robert Weiss, at Oldenburg. This Bf 109-equipped *Gruppe* had been relocated to Vendeville, in France, from the Eastern Front in February 1943. Once back in the West, its new duties including patrolling the French coast, until it was moved again late the following month, this time to Oldenburg, from where the *Gruppe* performed similar missions over the north German coast.

From June 1943 until May 1944, III./JG 54 engaged in such flights over the Dutch coast, in addition to patrolling German waters, until it received orders to relocate to Illesheim in May 1944 for operations in defence of the Reich. Following the Allied invasion, it was one of the aforementioned units despatched to France. Throughout the summer of 1944, III./JG 54 fought doggedly over France, but by mid-August, having suffered accumulating losses, the *Gruppe* was operating with a minimum number of pilots. On the 15th it was withdrawn, returning to Oldenburg, and reassigned as the first unit to receive the Fw 190D-9, the first four examples of which arrived from Rechlin on 20 September.

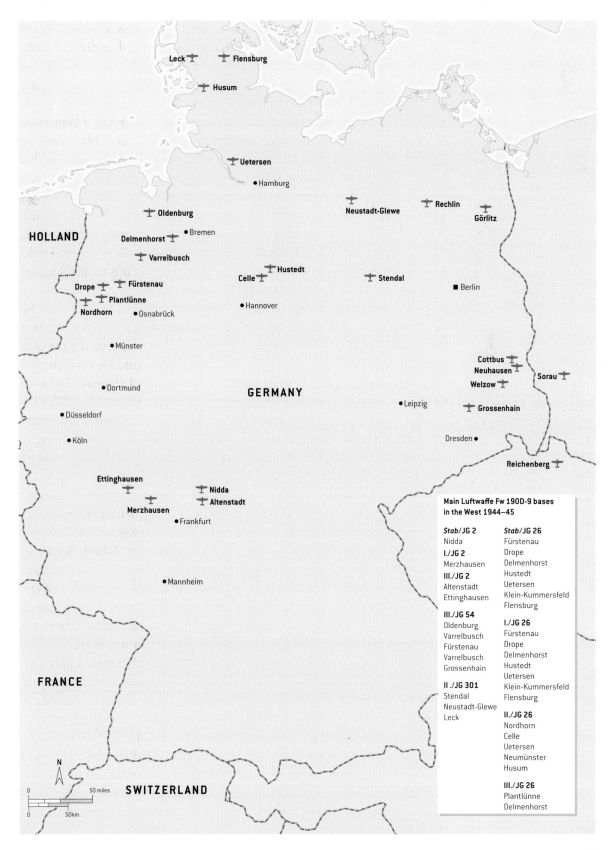

Leck Flensburg

Husum

Uetersen

● Hamburg

HOLLAND

Oldenburg

Delmenhorst ● Bremen

Varrelbusch

Neustadt-Glewe Rechlin

Görlitz

Celle Hustedt

Stendal

Drope Fürstenau

Plantlünne

Nordhorn ● Osnabrück

● Hannover

■ Berlin

● Münster

Cottbus

Neuhausen Sorau

Welzow

● Dortmund

GERMANY

● Leipzig Grossenhain

● Düsseldorf

● Köln

Dresden ●

Reichenberg

Ettinghausen

Nidda

Altenstadt

Merzhausen

● Frankfurt

Main Luftwaffe Fw 190D-9 bases in the West 1944–45

Stab/JG 2	*Stab*/JG 26
Nidda	Fürstenau
I./JG 2	Drope
Merzhausen	Delmenhorst
III./JG 2	Hustedt
Altenstadt	Uetersen
Ettinghausen	Klein-Kummersfeld
	Flensburg
III./JG 54	
Oldenburg	**I./JG 26**
Varrelbusch	Fürstenau
Fürstenau	Drope
Varrelbusch	Delmenhorst
Grossenhain	Hustedt
	Uetersen
II./JG 301	Klein-Kummersfeld
Stendal	Flensburg
Neustadt-Glewe	
Leck	**II./JG 26**
	Nordhorn
	Celle
	Uetersen
	Neumünster
	Husum
	III./JG 26
	Plantlünne
	Delmenhorst

● Mannheim

FRANCE

N

0   50 miles

0   50km

SWITZERLAND

15

The pilots of III./JG 54 were, initially, underwhelmed by the aircraft, with doubts expressed about its extended fuselage and new, heavier Jumo engine when compared to the shorter Fw 190A-8 and its compact BMW radial. However, that afternoon, once Hauptmann Weiss and his four *Staffelkapitäne* had flown the *'Langnase'* and experienced its superior rate-of-turn and faster rate-of-climb, opinions changed for the better. Two more D-9s were delivered on the 26th, and two days later, Weiss, a Knight's Cross-holder, demonstrated what could be achieved when, during the afternoon, he shot down the Spitfire PR XI flown by Flt Lt Duncan McCuaig of No 541 Sqn for his 119th aerial victory, and the first to be credited to the Fw 190D-9.

On 30 September, no less a figure than Kurt Tank visited Oldenburg. The designer and the pilots had the opportunity to discuss issues related to the new fighter, Tank stressing, as had his company's report in February 1944, that the D-9 should be regarded as an interim fighter intended to take advantage of the availability of the Jumo 213 following a decrease in demand for the engine in bombers. Production of the latter had been drastically curtailed, with priority now being given to fighters for defence of the Reich.

The OKL now wanted to get the new Focke-Wulf to operational units as fast as possible. As production went into full swing at Cottbus and Sorau, plans were made to manufacture four D-9s per day. They would be needed – and one of the most pressing requirements was to provide air cover for the Luftwaffe's new jet fighter and bomber units as they took off from, and returned to, their airfields in northwest Germany. Despite the unprecedented airspeeds of the Me 262 and Ar 234, the jets were at their most vulnerable to attack from enemy fighters during takeoff and landing.

September 1944 heralded the start of a wet, dismal autumn, as the troops and armour of Montgomery's 21st Army Group advanced steadily across Belgium to close on the port of Antwerp. Troops of the American Third Army had crossed the River Meuse in eastern France and were less than 100km from Germany. By late October Montgomery had reached the Scheldt, where the 21st Army Group was tasked with clearing the estuary of resistance so that Antwerp could be safely opened up to Allied shipping.

In mid-September, further to the east, the first American troops had crossed the Sauer river north of Trier and penetrated the frontier of the Reich itself. Two weeks later, elements of the American First Army breached what was thought to be the impenetrable Siegfried Line north of Aachen. The German Western Front was collapsing, and the Allies were now fighting within the borders of the Reich. Generalfeldmarschall Gerd von Rundstedt, the Commander-in-Chief West, signalled his troops, 'Soldiers of the Western Front! I expect you to defend Germany's sacred soil to the very last!'

On 7 November, II./JG 26 at Kirchhellen, under the command of Major Anton Hackl, was informed that it was to move to Reinsehlen to transition to the 'Dora'. The *Gruppe* was assigned 55 D-9s in December, and by the middle of the month II. *Jagdkorps* was demanding the unit quicken its training. On the 17th, the *Gruppe* moved into Nordhorn-Klausheide with 74 D-9s, as well as 20 freshly trained pilots. At Stendal, Hauptmann Herbert Nölter's II./JG 301 had received its first D-9s in early December, and shortly thereafter I. and III./JG 2 under Hauptmann Franz Hrdlicka and Hauptmann Siegfried Lemke, respectively, took delivery of 12 D-9s, with 53 'Doras' in place at III. *Gruppe*'s base at Ettinghausen towards the end the month.

But as the D-9 began to reach the Luftwaffe, so the Allied air forces continued to reinforce their fighter units and maintain pressure on the *Jagdwaffe*. Arrayed against the Luftwaffe throughout 1945 were 12 fighter and ground-attack wings of the 2nd TAF, numbering at any one time between 40–50 squadrons of Spitfire IXs, XIVs and XVIs, Typhoon IBs and Tempest Vs. Following the break-out from France, these aircraft had continued their support of Montgomery's forces across Belgium, the southern Netherlands and northwest Germany, undertaking armed reconnaissance, offensive patrols and fighter sweeps, during which they would clash with Luftwaffe fighters in the air, or attack them in strafing runs on the ground or wait over jet airfields.

In the autumn of 1944, P-38 Lightnings, P-47 Thunderbolts and P-51 Mustangs drawn from the 15 groups of the Eighth Air Force's three fighter wings also swarmed over northwest and central Germany as they escorted B-17 Flying Fortresses and B-24 Liberators on their strategic-level, large-scale bombing missions. With their charges safely shepherded out of enemy airspace, the fighter pilots routinely switched from 'defence' to 'offense' as they set about strafing ground targets on their way back to their bases in England.

Finally, the 15 fighter groups of the USAAF's Ninth Air Force carried out tactical rolling sweeps against airfields and transport targets from bases in France and Belgium. Indeed, many of the bases used by the 2nd TAF and Ninth Air Force had once been home to the Luftwaffe. Invariably, their new occupants found them bomb-damaged, sabotaged and littered with the wrecks of abandoned and shot-up German aircraft.

In crude terms, from September 1944 the stage was set for the mincing machine of Allied air power to take on the Fw 190D-9 units in what would be a fervent battle of attrition. Kurt Tank's design was to undergo its combat testing, as were its pilots.

CHAPTER 3
PATH TO COMBAT

By the time the first Fw 190D-9s reached the Luftwaffe in September 1944, the *Jagdwaffe*'s pilot training programme was under strain. The change from the pre-war training system, which was one of the finest in the world and which encouraged and provided careful, methodical instruction for a nation's youth on how to fly in both gliders and powered aircraft, to the hurried, constrained and disrupted methods in the autumn of 1944 could not have been more marked.

Nevertheless, despite a reduction in hours, fuel and instructors, as well as adverse operating conditions, pilots – even if less well prepared – continued to pass through a training process in 1943–44.

General reductions in the training programme meant that by the autumn of 1943, fighter pilots were reaching their operational units with an average of 148 hours on powered aircraft spread across an elementary A/B school, a Fighter Training School or *Jagdfliegerschule* and an *Ergänzungsjagdgruppe*

A wood-burning tractor pulls Fw 190D-9 Wk-Nr. 210051 across the apron by its locked tailwheel at Bremen-Neuenlanderfeld. The D-9, which was assigned to III./JG 54, has been fitted with a 300-litre drop tank for an extended range mission.
(EN Archive)

(Operational Fighter Training Group), compared to an average of 210 hours the previous year. An increase in non-combat losses thus reflected the pressures on fighter training.

Two young, future Fw 190D-9 pilots who commenced their flying training in 1942 were Gerhard Kroll and Heinz Radlauer, and their route to operations was typical of so many.

Radlauer was born in 1923, and as a teenager he learned to fly gliders around the Posen area. Typically, any boy attracted to aviation before and during the early years of the war would build model aircraft and then, if wanting to progress further, would enlist in his local 'Flying Hitler Youth' while still at school, where he was taught how to build and fly elementary plywood gliders such as the SG 38.

Sufficiently competent, the aspiring aviator set about obtaining the required three grades of the Civil Gliding Proficiency Badge (A, B and C) flying a Grunau Baby glider over the next five years. This involved five flights of 20 seconds each and one of 30 seconds (for A), five straight and level flights of 60 seconds (for B) and a final series of more lengthy flights (for C). Once a gliding badge had been earned, a candidate could then seriously start to contemplate service in the Luftwaffe.

After gaining his C-level qualification, Radlauer joined the Luftwaffe at the age of 17 in August 1941 and embarked upon basic military training in a *Fliegerausbildungsregiment* (Flying Training Regiment), where, as an aspiring air crew trainee, he underwent a standard course of 12 months comprising physical fitness training and 'culture', military discipline, routine medical examinations, basic infantry training, lectures on radio and communications, map reading and orienteering, aircraft recognition and sport.

Like Heinz Radlauer, Gerhard Kroll, who was born on 17 September 1924 in Elbing, West Prussia, also enlisted in the Luftwaffe in 1941 at the age of 17, and on 1 December that year was assigned to the 5. *Kompanie* of *Fliegerausbildungsregiment* 23 under Generalmajor Josef Putlar at Kaufbeuren, in the Allgäu region of southern Germany. In March 1942, Kroll was posted to 3. *Kompanie* of the *Luftwaffe Fliegeranwärterbataillon* (Cadet Battalion) III based at Straubing, southeast of Regensburg, under Oberst Karl-August von Blomberg. During his time with the battalion, which saw the unit relocated to Vannes, in western France, Kroll studied general aeronautical subjects.

Both trainees were accepted for military flying training and posted to a *Flugzeugführerschule* (FFS) A/B, where student pilots would

From gliders to the 'Dora' – Heinz Radlauer leans against the wing of Fw 190D-9 Wk-Nr 210097 'White 11' at the time of his surrender to British troops at Flensburg at the end of the war. This aircraft had been ferried, unarmed, from Köthen to Berlin-Gatow by Leutnant Walter Hagenah, a former Me 262 pilot with JG 7. Armament was added later. Radlauer was typical of so many future fighter pilots to pass through the Luftwaffe training system after the war had started. He would be credited with 15 victories, although none were scored during the 12 flights he made in the D-9. (Author)

After training in Germany and France, Unteroffizier Gerhard Kroll joined 9./JG 54 in February 1944 to fly Bf 109s. He converted to the D-9 in September 1944 and took part in airfield protection flights for the Me 262s of *Kommando Nowotny*. Kroll is credited with one victory – a B-17 on 8 March 1944 while he was flying a Bf 109 – although he was also shot down by return fire from the bomber. (Jerry Crandall Collection)

undertake courses to qualify for their powered aircraft certificates. In October 1941, Radlauer joined FFS A/B 61 at Oschatz, in eastern central Germany, under Oberstleutnant Philipp Neufang, while Kroll was sent to FFS A/B 14 under the command of Oberstleutnant Emil Becker at Klagenfurt, in Austria.

At *Flugzeugführerschule*, the student pilot would undertake a course to qualify for his powered aircraft certificates. The basic powered aircraft A1 certificate required that the trainee complete a loop, three landings without an error, an altitude flight to 2,000m and a 300km triangular flight course. All of these were to be accomplished in single- or two-seat aircraft weighing up to 500kg.

A2 certification was similar, except that it was for aircraft with at least two seats. Most pilots in the Luftwaffe trained on dual-control machines, so this, therefore, was the usual starter qualification. Following on from this was the B1 certificate. To obtain this, the student had to show that he had already achieved at least 3,000km of flight experience, completed a 600km triangular course in nine hours, undertaken an altitude flight to 4,500m, and made at least 50 flights in aircraft in the B1 category (single-engined one- to three-seater types with a maximum weight of 2,500kg). On top of this experience, the pilot had to carry out three precision landings, two night landings and a night flight lasting at least 30 minutes.

The requirements for the B2 certificate were progressively more difficult, requiring 6,000km of flight experience, including at least 3,000km in B1-category aircraft. In addition, 50 night flights were necessary, which had to include several difficult night landings.

Having gained an A/B certificate, the next posting for a trainee fighter pilot was to a *Jagdfliegerschule* (JFS – fighter school). Heinz Radlauer was assigned to JFS 7, under the command of Major Georg Meyer, in late 1942 at Nancy-Essay, in France. Here, he undertook initial fighter training, flying various obsolete or foreign fighter aircraft such as Ar 68 and He 51 biplanes and early-model Bf 109s, as well as assorted captured machines like the French D.520, before moving to existing operational types.

In early 1943 a major change within the Luftwaffe's fighter training infrastructure took place, and the *Jagdfliegerschulen* were placed on a semi-operational footing and redesignated as *Jagdgeschwader*. On 26 January 1943, JFS 7 became JG 107, the *Stab* and three component *Staffeln* of the *Schule* adopting the same designations as part of the new *Geschwader*. On 14 September 1943, Radlauer received his pilot's badge.

Likewise, Gefreiter Gerhard Kroll, who obtained his A/B certificate in January 1943, was posted to JFS 1, under the command of Oberstleutnant Otto-Friedrich Freiherr von Houwald, at Pau-Ost, in France. On 15 December 1942, this unit was redesignated as JG 101 and led by a veteran fighter pilot Oberstleutnant Erich von Selle. JG 101 comprised three *Staffeln*, each offering a self-contained training course of approximately 25 pupils and 20–25 aircraft – an assortment of Ar 96s, Bf 108s, Bf 109E/Fs and Bu 131s. A large proportion of the training was dedicated to formation flying, aerobatics, navigation, cross-country flying and gunnery practice.

In the summer of 1943, Kroll was promoted to Unteroffizier, and such was his apparent competence that JG 101 also made him an instructor (although this may not necessarily have involved flying).

In June 1944, Heinz Radlauer is believed to have been posted to *Ergänzungsjagdgruppe Ost* (Operational Training Fighter Group East), where operationally-experienced instructor pilots oversaw four-week-long courses intended to bring trained pilots to operational readiness in the Bf 109 and Fw 190 for service on the Eastern Front (similarly named *Ergänzungsjagdgruppen* were created for the *Süd* and *West* theatres). In reality, demands from the operational units shortened such courses to a duration of just 14 days.

During this short time pilots would complete circuits and bumps in a Bf 109F, followed by conversion, in the case of Radlauer, to the Bf 109G (or at the controls of a Bf 108 if converting to the Fw 190). Instruction in formation flying was similar to that received in a *Jagdfliegerschule*, but at least one flight was made in a seven- to nine-strong formation led by an instructor. Heavy emphasis was placed on gunnery training and target practice, using both machine guns and cannon.

After completion of this final course, Radlauer, who gained the somewhat derogatory nickname of *'Piefke'* (roughly 'Pipsqueak' – an Austrian slang expression for Germans of Prussian descent), was assigned to IV./JG 51, which was operating around the Minsk area in the central sector of the Eastern Front, in June 1944. For the past ten months the *Gruppe* had been under the command of Major Hans-Ekkehard Bob. When Bob had taken command of IV./JG 51, he found it to be suffering from heavy losses, as a result of which morale was not high. By the time Radlauer joined the *Gruppe*, command had recently changed to Major Heinz Lange.

Promoted to Feldwebel, Radlauer was now considered ready enough to take his place as a fully-fledged operational Bf 109G pilot. It is not clear which *Staffel* he served with, as sources have stated both 13. and 15./JG 51. The latter unit's first *Staffelkapitän* was the non-flying Leutnant Ernst Schmidt when it was formed at Modlin, in Poland, on 1 November 1943.

In January 1944, Gerhard Kroll was posted to the *Ergänzungsjagdgruppe* of JG 54 at Bayonne, training up on the Bf 109G and passing through this *Gruppe* within a matter of six or seven weeks. On 20 February,

Clad in flying gear, Oberleutnant Hans Dortenmann (centre), *Staffelkapitän* of 12./JG 54, and four fellow pilots from 11. and 12. *Staffeln* trudge through the snow at Varrelbusch in February 1945. (John Weal Collection)

Kroll was posted to 9./JG 54, based at Ludwigslust and equipped with Bf 109s for operations in the *Reichsverteidigung* (Defence of the Reich).

Thus Kroll, like many pilots who came to fly the D-9 in the closing months of the war, had already experienced aerial combat. His first contact with the enemy came on 8 March 1944, when, while engaging a USAAF B-17 that he claimed as shot down, his Messerschmitt was hit by return fire and he was forced to bail out. He subsequently spent a week on leave while he recovered from an injury to his ankle that he had sustained when he landed by parachute. Exactly a month later, Kroll was shot down again, his Bf 109G crash-landing in flames. Suffering third-degree burns, he was hospitalised in Lüneburg until the end of July 1944.

The following month, Kroll was posted to 1./*Jagdgruppe Ost* at Sagan, in Silesia, with whom he transitioned onto the Fw 190A-4 to A-8 variants. It was while he was undergoing familiarisation on the Focke-Wulf that his father, a Luftwaffe Feldwebel at Halberstadt airfield, was killed in an air raid on the base. Kroll was given compassionate leave to collect his father's effects and take them home to West Prussia. Then, on 9 September, he was reassigned to 9./JG 54 at Oldenburg under the command of Oberleutnant Willi Heilmann and in the process of converting to the Fw 190D-9.

It is probable that Kroll was one of the small number of pilots selected by two of III./JG 54's aces, Oberleutnant Hans Dortenmann, *Kapitän* of 12. *Staffel*, and Leutnant Peter Crump of 10. *Staffel*, who had been despatched by *Gruppenkommandeur* Hauptmann Weiss to *Jagdgruppe Ost* at Sagan to select suitable candidates to fly the new 'Dora'. Unfortunately, both Dortenmann and Crump were utterly dismayed by what they saw at Sagan. The standard of training was alarming, with the student pilots lacking sufficient flying experience as a result of hurried instruction. They were thus also lacking in confidence, and in no way prepared for what lay ahead of them in the skies over the Western Front.

This was symptomatic of the Luftwaffe's position by late 1944, and it was beginning to show. Yet, in mid-November, Reichsmarschall Hermann Göring, commander-in-chief of the Luftwaffe, had ordered II. *Jagdkorps* 'to attack enemy fighter-bombers at airfields near the frontline' and even more importantly 'to fly fighter cover for the Army to give it freedom of movement'. But the commander of the *Korps*, Generalmajor Dietrich Peltz, had become increasingly concerned as reports reached him of *jagdflieger* breaking off engagements with enemy fighters without good reason and jettisoning drop tanks to race back to the relative safety of Reich airspace.

Fuel was still available in reasonable quantities for frontline units, but a shortage was beginning to impinge on the training schools, affecting standards. By late 1944, fuel stocks for training were at their lowest levels, resulting in standard training being slashed from 260 hours per pupil to about 50. Even the best instructors were unable to work miracles with so few hours at their disposal. In the *Ergänzungsgruppen*, only 20 tons of fuel was available for each pilot. This equated to just 25 hours of flying per pupil – much less than their RAF counterparts.

In III./JG 54, Weiss and his executive officers endeavoured to maintain some kind of effective training regime, particularly when bad weather curtailed flying and young pilots grew bored. If possible, daily lectures were held on tactics, including low-level attacks, gunnery and target training, flying and formation discipline, and radio technique. They were also required to watch the mechanics and armourers at work so that they could obtain a real understanding of how the 'Dora' functioned.

Oberleutnant Dortenmann noted in his diary on 20 October (Jakl, *Dortenmann*):

> I hound my *Staffel* to fly as many practice missions as possible. We fly in any weather. They have given me freedom of action. In a short period of time I mould the *Staffel* into a fighting unit, train my *Rotten* and *Schwarm* leaders and look with a little more confidence to the future.

In the Fw 190D-9, Kurt Tank achieved a design that combined a sense of purpose with elegance. Factory-fresh production example Wk-Nr. 210051 was assigned to III./JG 54, the first Luftwaffe fighter unit to equip with the 'Dora' in September 1944. (EN Archive)

In the East, 'Piefke' Radlauer is believed to have been credited with his first victory on 7 October 1944 when he shot down a La-5 fighter while flying the Bf 109G. He gained his second, over a Yak-9, six days later, and was credited with his third, an Il-2, on 14 October. 15./JG 51 would remain

This Fw 190D-9 Wk-Nr. 211132 was a machine from the second Focke-Wulf production batch of 290 aircraft. The date of *5.12.44* hand-applied to the cowling was probably its completion or delivery date. It is believed the aircraft went on to be assigned to the *Gruppenstab* of JG 11, with whom the fighter served as 'Black 4' until it was destroyed when it hit an obstacle shortly after take-off from Strausberg airfield on 8 February 1945. The pilot, Oberfähnrich Walter Krist, was killed. (EN Archive)

at Modlin until 23 January 1945, when it relocated to Danzig-Langfuhr, by which time the *Staffel* was under the leadership of Hauptmann Hellmuth Scheuber, the former *Adjutant* of I. *Gruppe*. In total, IV. *Gruppe* had claimed 102 victories during the course of the previous month at Modlin, and in return had had four pilots killed and two wounded. By then, Feldwebel Radlauer had been credited with three confirmed victories and had been awarded the Iron Cross First Class. He had himself been shot down on one occasion.

However, the airfield at Danzig-Langfuhr faced continual Soviet bombardment and shelling, and operations from there became impossible. A further change of base occurred when the *Staffel* pulled back along the Baltic coast to Anklam on 20 March, by which point Radlauer had increased his tally to seven victories with the destruction of two Yak-9s, an Il-2 and a La-5. Another move followed in April, this time to Garz, on the island of Usedom.

In the last chaotic weeks of the war, as a member of Oberleutnant Kurt Tanzer's 13./JG 51, Radlauer 'converted' to the Fw 190A, this comprising a quick explanation of the instruments by a representative of Focke-Wulf as the pilot sat in the cockpit! Subsequently, he received the most rudimentary training on the Fw 190D-9 when a small number of machines were delivered to IV./JG 51 on 16 April. He flew the D-9 for the first time four days later, and on 22 April Radlauer claimed two Yak-3s shot down while flying a 'Dora', although these successes remained unconfirmed.

It is a telling irony that despite Focke-Wulf delivering a new fighter which was comparable to the latest Allied types, and despite its pressing need by the *Jagdgruppen*, production was insufficient, as was the extent and quality of training for the pilots assigned to fly it.

CHAPTER 4
WEAPON OF WAR

Focke-Wulf chief test pilot Flugkapitän Hans Sander made the first flight in the first production Fw 190D-9 Wk-Nr. 210001 TR+SA from the firm's Sorau works on 31 August 1944, and the machine was then used by the company for long-term testing. It would be fitted with two Rheinmetall-Borsig 13mm MG 131 machine guns above the engine and two Mauser 20mm MG 151/20E cannon in the wing roots. The second production aircraft, Wk-Nr. 210002 TR+SB, was flown for the first time by Hauptmann Schmitz, a representative from the *Erprobungsstelle* Rechlin, on 15 September.

As testing progressed, some problems were noted, mainly associated with the Jumo 213 engine – not necessarily in terms of performance, but more in regard to build and finish. According to an assessment made by Focke-Wulf engineers at Langenhagen, 'substantial gaps' were found to be present in the engine, particularly where the cowling met the wing. This resulted in adjustment of the lower cowling against the propeller rotation

A pristine Fieseler-built Fw 190D-9 of II./JG 26, probably recently delivered and purportedly photographed at Reinsehlen, although the *Gruppe* had left that base by mid-August 1944. The aircraft is fitted with a 300-litre drop tank and has a heavily mottled camouflage scheme. (EN Archive)

direction, since issues had arisen from engine torque in flight. The fairing was sealed using rubber gaskets and metal strips. Generally, such issues were not uncommon to most new aircraft at this early stage of development.

However, in assessing the Fw 190D-9 when it reached frontline units, Leutnant Karl-Heinz Ossenkop, a pilot from 2./JG 26, recalled (Crandall, *Fw 190 Dora*, pg 60–61):

> I was struck by the high quality of my new mount. The joints of aluminium sheeting and the riveting were very smooth, helping to reduce drag. Overall, we pilots of JG 26 were very pleased with these new machines. Yes, we were doubtful at first, but we became more confident, and felt we were at least equal, or, in some cases, even better, allowing us to win the battle in a Fw 190D-9.

In fairness, intended as an interim solution pending arrival of the Ta 152 fighter, Focke-Wulf always saw the Fw 190D-9 being delivered in limited quantities, and with the minimum number of changes in design from the radial-engined Fw 190A in order to minimise costs. Nevertheless, from the autumn of 1944, production of the Fw 190D-9 expanded to include the Focke-Wulf plants at Cottbus and Sorau, and license-built production block manufacture by a consortium known as the *Arbeitsgemeinschaft Roland*. The latter was overseen by Weser Flugzeugbau (Weserflug) at Nordenham (which made fuselages), while the Gerhard Fieseler Werke at Kassel-Waldau and the Mitteldeutsche Metallwerke (Mimetall or MME) at Erfurt-Nord were also brought in.

Weserflug had a long-standing relationship with Junkers dating back to before the war, as did the Allgemeine Transportanlagen GmbH (ATG) at Leipzig and the Siebel Flugzeugwerke at Halle. Under the umbrella of the Focke-Wulf-controlled '*Sonderausschuss* (Special Committee) F4', these firms brought their collective assets, skills and manufacturing capabilities together to accelerate D-9 production. Junkers (at Bernburg), Siebel (at Halle) and

An NCO, with the cloth badge of the flight technical service on his lower sleeve, photographed in front of newly arrived, late-production Fw 190D-9s for JG 6 in February 1945. The aircraft had been flown in from the Focke-Wulf plant at Sorau. (EN Archive)

On 1 January 1945, Leutnant Theo Nibel of 10./JG 54 took part in Operation *Bodenplatte*, attacking the Allied airfield at Grimbergen. However, his Sorau-built D-9, Wk-Nr. 210079 'Black 12', suffered a bird strike and he was forced to land near Wemmel. Nibel's 'Dora' would be the first D-9 captured by the Allies. Here, the engine cover panels are lifted to reveal the Jumo 213 cradled by its bearers, as well as the auxiliary coolant tank (forward) and oil tank (to rear). The aircraft was photographed in February 1945 after it had been transported to the Royal Aircraft Establishment at Farnborough for examination. (EN Archive)

Union (at Hameln) would supply wings and undercarriage doors, fuselage and wing sections, and landing gear components, respectively, to Junkers at Gotha for assembly. They would be joined by ATG supplying rear fuselages and tail units, Kopperschmidt at Blumberg making canopies, and Focke-Wulf at Posen building ailerons and flaps.

Forty D-9s were delivered from Sorau in September, followed by 70 in October and 142 in November. Fieseler came on stream in October, producing 41 aircraft by the end of the following month. In total, 366 Fw 190D-9s had been delivered by 30 November, with output reaching 716 aircraft by year-end. Production peaked in January 1945 with 1,030 machines being delivered, the bulk (172) being made by Focke-Wulf – Mimetall also produced 64 that month.

It is believed that 172 of the machines produced in January were D-9/R11 all-weather variants with appropriate technical equipment installed, while another 28 were delivered fitted with the EZ 42 reflector gunsight.

When it came to operational performance, the D-9 introduced two advantages to Luftwaffe fighter pilots. Firstly, the fitment of the Jumo 213, and the resulting sleeker aerodynamic design associated with the V12 engine, meant that the new fighter was 28km/h faster that the more rounded, radial-engined Fw 190A-8 at low-level.

Leutnant Ossenkop remembered (Hermann, *Fw 190 'Long Nose'*, pg 119):

In general, I should say that we of the I./JG 26 *'Schlageter'* were very satisfied with the D-9, and regretted that this aircraft had not appeared at the front much sooner. The old Fw 190A-8 that we flew until 24 December 1944 was surely no feast for the eyes compared to the Bf 109, the Spitfire or the P-51D Mustang, with their elegant lines. The A-8 was powered by a bulky BMW 801 radial engine and tapered to the rear like a tadpole. The lengthened fuselage of the Fw 190D-9 transformed the aircraft and placed it in the same class as the abovementioned machines.

Two semi-circular coolant radiators were mounted around the reduction gear casing in a circular cowling, to the rear of which were annular gills that were automatically controlled by a thermostat mounted at the top of the engine crankcase. The gills could be adjusted alternately by a control in the cockpit. The company noted in its description of the aircraft in December 1943, "No engine-mounted cannon has been fitted, although the engine is designed to allow the later installation of the MK 108 [but not the MK 103!]. For reasons of stability, a 500mm section has been fitted in the rear fuselage. This partly compensates for the aircraft's nose-heaviness resulting from the installation of the heavier engine. Depending on the equipment installed in the aircraft, between 10kg and 30kg of ballast has to be affixed in the vertical stabiliser."

Furthermore, emergency power was increased to 1,900hp at altitudes up to 5,000m as part of a *Sonderaktion* (special action) feature at lower ceilings – a blessing for less experienced pilots when pitted against a Spitfire, Tempest V or P-51. This was particularly important given the low-level mission profiles which were undertaken by the D-9, such as jet airfield cover and low-level ground-attack runs.

Secondly, and as described in Chapter 2, the incorporation of an MW 50 power-boosting system. This increased speed at 5,700m to 702km/h; a margin of 17km/h, and in a climb this represented an increase from a standard 18.8m/sec to 22.5m/sec with MW 50 boost. In theory at least, these figures matched those of the Griffon-engined Spitfire XIV.

In February 1945, 25-year-old Sudeten-born Oberleutnant Oskar Romm got the chance to put the Fw 190D-9 through its paces when examples of the aircraft were issued to IV./JG 3 – he was the unit's *Gruppenkommandeur*. Romm had joined the Luftwaffe in 1939 and commenced flight training as a fighter pilot in July 1941. He was subsequently assigned to 1./JG 51 in the East, and from early 1943 his confirmed victory claims rose impressively. Romm was credited with multiple victories on one day with JG 51 on no fewer than 18 occasions between 24 February 1943 and 5 February 1944. On 14 August he was credited with downing five Soviet aircraft, and six days later he accounted for six. On 5 February 1944, he was credited with four P-39s, a Boston medium bomber and a Yak-9 shot down.

It is believed Romm's service with JG 51 was interrupted for a period in mid-1943 when he was assigned as an instructor with the *Ergänzungsjagdgruppe Ost* in France, possibly with the dual intention of providing him with some rest from the front and also to benefit new pilots with his experience. He was awarded the Knight's Cross with the rank of Oberfeldwebel on 29 February 1944, having been credited with 76 victories.

From early July 1944, Romm became proficient as an anti-bomber pilot, having been transferred firstly to 11. and then 12.(*Sturm*)/JG 3. He is credited with shooting down four B-24s and four B-17s between 7 July and 29 September. In late 1944, Romm is believed to have then had a spell of leadership with 4./JG 3 and the *Stab* I./EJG 1, before being appointed *Staffelkapitän* of the Fw 190-equipped 15.(*Sturm*)/JG 3 on 15 January 1945, which transferred from Gütersloh in quick succession to Markisch-Friedland and then Stargard on the 25th. His tally by then stood at 86 victories.

The IV. *Gruppe* of JG 3 would start to receive the Fw 190D-9 in February, and on the 17th of that month Romm was propelled into command of the whole *Gruppe* when the incumbent *Kommandeur*, Major Erwin Bacsila, was transferred to the Me 163-equipped JG 400.

Romm recalled (Price, *At War*, pg 132–133):

I first saw the 'Dora-9' in December 1944 at Stargard, near Stettin. The aircraft had just been delivered from the Focke-Wulf works at Marienburg, near Danzig in East Prussia. From Stargard, our task was to mount bombing and strafing attacks against Russian forces advancing towards Berlin and Stettin.

I was very keen to get hold of the Fw 190D-9 because I could see that before long we should be engaged in a war on two fronts against, on the one side the Russians and, on the other, the British and American fighters and bombers. For such fighting I considered the D-9 to be the ideal aircraft. I succeeded in getting one full *Staffel* equipped with this version, as well as my *Gruppe Stab* with four of these aircraft plus one reserve. To get some of the aircraft we had to rescue them from airfields that were about to be overrun by the enemy, in spite of all the risks involved.

All of our *Dora*-9s were fitted with the Jumo 213A engine which, with water methanol injection, developed 2,240 horsepower. As an air superiority fighter, the Fw 190D-9 handled better than the Fw 190A; it was faster and had a superior rate of climb. During dogfights at altitudes of between 3,050m and 7,300m, usual when engaging the Russians, I found that I could pull the Fw 190D into a tight turn and still retain my speed advantage. In the Fw 190A I had flown previously, during dogfights I had often to reduce to minimum flying speed in the turn. In the descent the *Dora*-9 picked up speed much more rapidly than the A-type; in the dive it could leave the Russian Yak-3 and Yak-9 fighters standing.

Romm also stated (Grinsell, *Focke-Wulf Fw 190*, pg 47–48) that the D-9 was, quite simply:

. . . the fastest prop-driven aircraft I have ever flown. It was supplied with a gyro-stabilised *Revi* 16b reflector gunsight, and with this sight I found I could hit the cockpit of a Russian DB-7 from a very great distance. The Fw 190D-9 included all the good qualities of the regular Fw 190, with a higher speed and a higher climb rate. It also included a MW 50 injection system that not only boosted power output, but also reduced engine temperatures under high rpm situations.

Although Unteroffizier Heinz Gehrke of III./JG 26 agreed with Romm in respect to the speed of the D-9, he remained an advocate of the Bf 109 (Caldwell, *Top Guns*, pg 355):

The 'Dora-9' was a wild bird. Everything was electric. Landing gear, flaps and trim tabs needed only the press of a button. And the bird was fast! In the 109 we could hit 500–520km/h at low altitude, fully armed and equipped – the D-9 was a good 50–60 km/h faster. However, for pure flying, I preferred the Messerschmitt, despite all of its problems during take-off and landing.

There was also a plan to equip the D-9s built by Fieseler with a GM 1 boost for high-altitude flying, but the RLM (*Reichsluftfahrtministerium* – Ministry of Aviation) decided to defer this until the introduction of the intended D-12 and D-13 variants. The *General der Jagdflieger*, Generalmajor Adolf Galland, was not an enthusiast of the GM 1 system, reasoning that the nitrous oxide mixture could evaporate on warm days when aircraft were sat waiting on airfields.

Two 87–90 octane self-sealing fuel tanks were installed in the D-9's fuselage, with the forward tank holding 230 litres and the aft tank holding 290 litres (totalling 520 litres). There were two interconnected oil tanks

This graphic from Focke-Wulf's Fw 190D-9 handbook shows the aircraft's armament, comprising two fuselage-mounted 13mm MG 131 machine guns (1) forward of the cockpit and two 20mm MG 151/20E cannon in the wings (2). Note also the Revi 16B reflector gunsight (15) and the ammunition cannisters (8 and 21). (EN Archive)

I. Beschreibung der Schußwaffenanlage der Baureihe D-9

A. Allgemeines

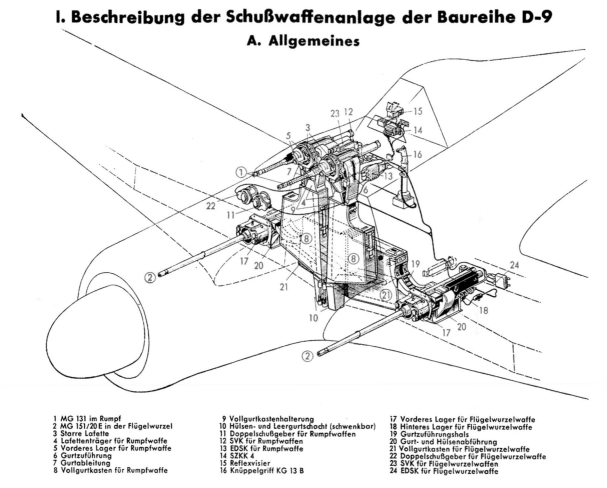

1 MG 131 im Rumpf	9 Vollgurtkastenhalterung	17 Vorderes Lager für Flügelwurzelwaffe
2 MG 151/20 E in der Flügelwurzel	10 Hülsen- und Leergurtschacht (schwenkbar)	18 Hinteres Lager für Flügelwurzelwaffe
3 Starre Lafette	11 Doppelschußgeber für Rumpfwaffen	19 Gurtzuführungshals
4 Lafettenträger für Rumpfwaffe	12 SVK für Rumpfwaffen	20 Gurt- und Hülsenabführung
5 Vorderes Lager für Rumpfwaffe	13 EDSK für Rumpfwaffe	21 Vollgurtkasten für Flügelwurzelwaffe
6 Gurtzuführung	14 SZKK 4	22 Doppelschußgeber für Flügelwurzelwaffe
7 Gurtableitung	15 Reflexvisier	23 SVK für Flügelwurzelwaffen
8 Vollgurtkasten für Rumpfwaffe	16 Knüppelgriff KG 13 B	24 EDSK für Flügelwurzelwaffe

Abb. 1: Gesamtbild der Schußwaffenanlage

Fw 190D-9 ARMAMENT

The Fw 190D-9 fielded a pair of fuselage-mounted, belt-fed, air-cooled Rheinmetall-Borsig 13mm MG 131 machine guns firing at a rate of 900 rounds per minute (475 rounds per gun). The ammunition containers for the machine guns were located directly beneath the guns. The 'Dora' was also armed with a pair of Mauser 20mm MG 151/20E wing-mounted, recoil-operated, belt-fed cannon firing at a rate of 780 rounds per minute (250 rounds per gun), one weapon mounted in each wing root. Their ammunition containers were housed just forward of the cockpit.

of 35 litres and 25 litres at the rear of the engine on the port side. Oil was fed from the lower tank to the pressure pump on the engine. It was collected by a scavenger pump and delivered to the oil cooler, which it passed through to a metal, disk-type, dual filter, the elements of which could be rotated by means of a lever. From the filter the oil was returned to the top oil tank, thus completing the circuit. The oil cooler, through which the coolant passed, was of the cylindrical type.

Standard armament for the D-9 comprised two 13mm MG 131 machine guns (with 475 rounds per gun in the fuselage) and two 20mm MG 151/20E (with 250 rounds per gun in the wing roots) cannon. The spacing between the two MG 131s had to be increased from 260mm to 308mm on account of the position of the synchroniser on the Jumo 213. Research in recent years has revealed that there were variations in the shape of the aerodynamically streamlined cowling designed to cover the MG 131 fuselage guns. The cowling was designed to be opened using four fastening clips, and was hinged to raise upwards just in front of the canopy windscreen.

The other engine cowlings were Junkers-made, and part of the overall 'power egg'. They featured a gentle bulge at the rear to house the MG 131s' electrical ammunition feed mechanism, but eventually they became unnecessary. Nevertheless, sub-contractors and satellite factories such as Weserflug, Mimetall and Fieseler produced their own versions of the cowling in front of the windscreen which varied in the number of panels used in their construction, as well as their 'bulges' and flairs.

Most other equipment was taken from the Fw 190A-8 series, with minor changes associated mainly with the installation of the Jumo 213.

Karl-Heinz Ossenkop recalled (Hermann, *Fw 190 'Long Nose'*, pg 118–119):

Fw 190D-9 'White 1' assigned to 5./JG 26 is seen in the spring of 1945 after it was flown to Norway. Note the highly unusual fitment of two underwing racks, each for 13 55mm R4M rockets, immediately outboard of the undercarriage legs. These were probably intended for use in ground-attack missions against Allied motorised transport, rather than for shooting down aircraft. This was a rare fitment, and it is believed to have been used by only a few aircraft of JG 26. Note also the later style, 170-litre cylindrical drop tank. (EN Archive)

We began converting to the Fw 190D-9 in Fürstenau on 24 December 1944. From then until 31 December we had the opportunity to familiarise ourselves with the new machine and fly training missions. The first problems cropped up when the machines were test flown. In several cases the ignition cut out during a steep, banking turn to the left. There was general consternation: 'What are we to do with such a bird?' It was inevitable that the pilots should have reservations about the new machine. Civilian engineers from Junkers soon came to the rescue.

When filled with belted ammunition for the left MG 131 above the engine, the metal ammunition tank located in the front of the firewall pressed on the system of cables from the generator to the engine. The problem had obviously not made itself felt during unarmed factory test flights. The field workshop came up with a solution: a metal spacer which was riveted in place. I don't know if the Junkers people submitted a modification report to the BAL [Construction Supervisory Board, Air] – that was not my concern. All I know for sure is that it is a dangerous affair to have a fighter strapped to your behind whose engine splutters or stops every now and then. Once this problem was cleared up, there were scarcely any complaints about the new bird.

As he sat in the cockpit of the Fw 190D-9, the pilot looked ahead through a 50mm-thick armoured glass central windscreen flanked by 30mm left and right side window panels. Beneath the central screen was an instrument panel that was well laid out and crowned by a Revi (*Reflexvisier*) 16B reflector gunsight. Directly below this and to the left was a SSZK 4 armament switch and control panel, while to the right was the AFN 2 homing indicator for the FuG 16ZY VHF direction-finding radio transceiver. The gun-firing buttons and a bomb release button were mounted on the Knüppelgriff KG 13B control column.

The main instrument panel contained three tiers of gauges. The airspeed indicator, artificial horizon, rate of climb/descent indicator and supercharger pressure gauge were below the SSZK 4 and AFN 2. In the lower tier were the fuel and oil pressure and oil and coolant temperature gauges, the propeller pitch indicator, fuel gauge and warning lights. To the pilot's left was a console containing the throttle and undercarriage controls and the switches for the FuG 16ZY. To his right was the console containing a clock, flare box cover and fuel, pump and armament circuit breaker switches.

Beyond the firewall/bulkhead were the four large containers housing the ammunition for the port and starboard MG 131s and MG 151/20Es, respectively.

Oberleutnant Hans Hartigs flew the 'Dora' with 4./JG 26. Twenty-five years old in the spring of 1945, he had joined JG 26 from training in July 1943. Flying with 2. *Staffel*, Hartigs had claimed his first victory on 29 January 1944 when he shot down a P-38 of the 20th Fighter Group (FG) in the Saarbrücken–Koblenz area, and claimed his fifth success to attain ace status on 26 July. The following month he was shot down by

These two Fw 190D-9s were possibly photographed at Welzow in 1945. The aircraft in the foreground has been identified as the mount of Oberfeldwebel Max Sulzgruber of 6./JG 301. Both fighters have two-colour Reich defence identification bands around their rear fuselages, which could be the yellow/red marking unique to JG 301. The aircraft in the foreground is ready for operations, with a 300-litre drop tank fitted. A pilot's parachute also lies on the horizontal stabiliser. (EN Archive)

P-47s near Paris, suffering injuries when he bailed out of his Fw 190A. Hartigs would not rejoin the *Geschwader* until November, just as JG 26 commenced training on the new D-9. He was not a convert (Eriksson, *Alarmstart*, pg 214):

The Fw 190D-9 *'Langnase'* I did not enjoy flying: I found earlier types much better in dogfights and turning ability. The engine in the D-model in fact ran more roughly, and it was very insensitive when shooting.

In 1946 USAAF Materiel Command test pilots flew a captured D-9, and concluded that:

The Fw 190D-9, although well armoured and equipped to carry heavy armament, appears to be much less desirable from a handling standpoint than other models of the Fw 190 using the BMW 14-cylinder radial engine. Any advantage that this aircraft may have in performance over other models of the Fw 190 is more than offset by its poor handling characteristics.

Conversely, another D-9 pilot, Hauptmann Roderich Cescotti, who commanded II./JG 301 based at Stendal, Neustadt-Glewe and Leck, felt that the 'Dora' was a 'splendid machine' which suffered from few technical failures. In his view, the greatest challenge facing the aircraft, and those that flew it, was a lack of fuel in the Third Reich by early 1945.

CHAPTER 5

ART OF WAR

In the last quarter of 1944 and into 1945, it was usual for Fw 190D-9 pilots to begin their day by being transported from their billets in local private houses or barracks, which could be several kilometres away from their unit's airfield, by whatever form of transport was available – often a military or requisitioned civilian bus.

Either at their quarters or once they reached the airfield, depending on the unit and base, they would make their way to their mess and partake of a breakfast that would comprise, typically, *ersatz* (substitute) coffee with some bread and jam and occasionally an egg. Pilots preferred to eat food that would not cause intestinal gas, which could cause discomfort and distraction at altitude.

They would then head across the airfield to their wooden readiness huts. These were usually assigned on a *Staffel* by *Staffel* basis, as *Staffeln* were often distributed around an airfield, and each would have its own hut for its pilots. In the case of II./JG 26 at Nordhorn, for example, 5. *Staffel*, regarded as the 'alert' *Staffel* and the first to take off on any large-scale missions, was quartered at the western end of the airfield, while the other *Staffeln* were at the eastern end.

The *Gruppe* staff would be housed in the *Gefechtsstand* (command post), from where daily orders, mission instructions and meteorological and intelligence information would be relayed to the component *Staffeln*. As they waited for the events of the day to break, the pilots would discuss with their *Staffelkapitän* who would fly in which position, run over formation organisation and discipline, radio communication procedures, likely targets, known enemy activity and so on. If the autumn or spring sun shone, *Staffel*-level briefings could take place outside.

Once discussion had been exhausted, clad in their black leather flying gear and fur-lined boots, they would – as had so many fighter pilots before

Mechanics undertake work on an Fw 190D-9 of 3./JG 26 parked in its wooded dispersal at Fürstenau in February 1945. A later-type 170-litre drop tank is fitted to the centreline rack, behind which can be seen the aerial for the FuG 16ZY VHF transceiver. (EN Archive)

them of all belligerents – typically sit in old chairs or deckchairs, weather allowing, outside their wooden readiness huts in a mixture of tiredness and tense expectation. Some tried their best to read, others managed to doze, and a few would play cards. A few pilots who found the waiting too difficult would go over to their aircraft to check it or to talk with the mechanics, perhaps to ascertain whether a fault or leak had been fixed from the previous day. It was a relief when the music piped through the loud speakers stopped and the time came to climb into cockpits. The process of pulling on a parachute pack, fastening straps, closing a canopy, starting up an engine, switching on sights and checking instruments became a familiar sanctuary to many.

When ordered to fly by the *Jagddivision*, instructions would be relayed from the *Gefechtsstand* to the waiting pilots by loudspeaker to prepare them for take-off in 30 minutes.

After a final map briefing with the *Staffelkapitän*, who would have also discussed the mission with the *Kommandeur*, the pilots made their way to their aircraft, which had been warmed up and readied by the mechanics and armourers. The more experienced pilots and officers tended to retain their own aircraft. As Gerhard Kroll, a pilot with III./JG 54, commented, 'It is like with horses; each aeroplane has his characteristics. If one knows them, you get along better.'

By this stage of the war, it was usual for the D-9s to be dispersed, sheltered and hidden in woods around the airfield. As, for example, at III./JG 54's base at Varrelbusch, aircraft were pushed into the trees tail-first and covered with fir branches. Black-overalled mechanics and armourers would subsequently carry out maintenance on their charges in such austere conditions. At I./JG 26's base at Fürstenau, the 'Doras' were simply rolled into gaps amongst some spindly pines, but even so, the groundcrews had turned the use of tree branches and leaves into a camouflage art form.

Ahead of the pilots' arrival, and where used, tree branches and natural foliage or camouflage netting would be pulled away from the aircraft by the groundcrews. The pilots would take their place in the cockpit of their assigned machine, with parachute and flare pistol waiting. The *jagdflieger* had only to fasten his parachute and seat harnesses, switch on the radio set and plug into the oxygen system.

By early 1945, the Luftwaffe could not afford to allow its fighters to remain open to attack on airfields with no concealment or protection. In a scene common to other airfields throughout Germany, Fw 190D-9s of 7./JG 26, led at the time by Oberleutnant Gottfried Schmidt, emerge from their wooded dispersal at Nordhorn-Klausheide at the start of another patrol in February 1945. (EN Archive)

'Taxi-tracks' were little more than slightly widened forest tracks on which were laid, occasionally, logs or planks, to provide some assistance to movement amidst the often rutted grass and sand surface which could become soft and muddy after heavy rain. Movement was all but impossible without the aid of the groundcrews, who would do their best to guide the pilots, one after the other, through the gloom of the woods from the edge of the tracks, deafened by the noise of the Jumo engines and their faces coated by dust. On the ground, from way back in his cockpit, the pilot had only limited visibility over the 'long nose' of the 'Dora'. Sometimes, as for example at II./JG 26's airfield at Nordhorn, the unit's mechanics would sit on the forward edge of the wings of their D-9s to assist in guiding them out.

As a prudent measure intended to minimise risk, on 25 March 1945 – the day II./JG 26 was to transfer from Nordhorn to Bissel – *Gruppenkommandeur* Hauptmann Paul Schauder ordered the *Gruppe*'s more experienced pilots to take off first so that in the case of any accidents they would not be held back on the ground. This proved insightful, for two Focke-Wulfs did collide with the loss of two aircraft and two pilots from 5./JG 26. In addition, the *Geschwader* lost a pilot from 3. *Staffel* when his aircraft struck a tree, while another from 11. *Staffel* hit a crater on landing at Delmenhorst, the D-9 overturning and its pilot suffering minor injuries.

On a more typical day of operations, the Focke-Wulf pilots would taxi into their assigned *Staffel* positions from their various dispersal points, joining up with their comrades with whom they would fly in respective *Rotten* and *Schwärme* formations. This was a dangerous time, for the fighters would be massed on the ground in the open, forming an unmissable target for preying Allied fighters. Never was airfield Flak so important.

Colour-coded signal pistols were fired, and at a distance of 150–200m, pair after pair of aircraft would roll towards the runway. 'This was not without danger', Unteroffizier Werner Molge of 7./JG 26 recalled, 'because of the propwash from the preceding aircraft. If one was caught in the wash at the moment of lift-off, it could make an awful mess.'

Furthermore, out on the runways, the surfaces were often left damaged by Allied air attacks. All available personnel would be used to fill in bomb craters with sand, usually during the hours of darkness.

Generally, the D-9 units adhered to the long-established, tried and tested *Rotte* and *Schwarm* formations. The standard four-aircraft *Schwarm* fighter formation evolved from the earlier three-aircraft *Kette* used by pilots of the *Legion Condor* during the Spanish Civil War. High-scoring early war ace Werner Mölders was a leading proponent of the *Schwarm*, and he duly refined and exploited it, and pushed for the formation's adoption by the *Jagdwaffe*.

A four-aircraft formation was found to offer greater in-flight cohesion and tactical flexibility. The *Schwarm* comprised two pairs – *Rotten* – in which one wingman, positioned behind, monitored and guarded the *Rottenführer's* (lead pilot's) course. The two *Rotten* flew in a loose line abreast formation, but with the rear *Rotte* echeloned back so that effectively the wingman concept extended by *Rotte* to the whole *Schwarm* and resulted in a 'finger-four' formation, broadly resembling the fingers of an outstretched hand.

Radio communication, where possible, also aided formation control and situational awareness. Generally, it was found that the best distance between aircraft was around 180–200m. By scanning the sky inwards, blind spots below and behind could be covered. Quick turning was accomplished by the lead aircraft of the lead *Rotte* climbing and turning 90 degrees first, with his wingman following, followed by the rear *Rotte*, to result in a mirror/reverse line, but with formation cohesion retained.

When radio communication was not available, or if it failed, pilots would resort to hand signals to indicate if a fellow pilot had moved in too close while in formation.

Larger formations would, in turn, be comprised of several *Schwärme*, with a lead *Schwarm* flying slightly ahead and other *Schwarm* positioned on either side, the one to the right staggered slightly further back. In the

A member of the groundcrew watches as two Fw 190D-9s from 7./JG 26 taxi out from their forested dispersal at Nordhorn-Klausheide in February 1945. Timber planks have been thrown down haphazardly to aid traction on the soft ground conditions for the 'Doras'. (EN Archive)

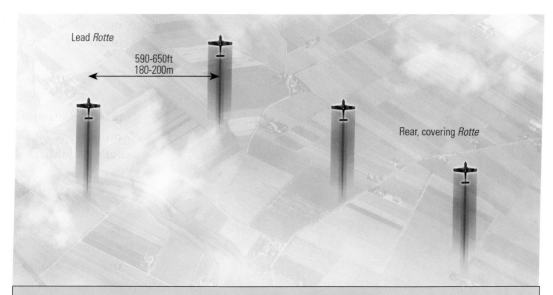

Lead *Rotte*

590-650ft
180-200m

Rear, covering *Rotte*

'FINGER-FOUR' FORMATION

The standard four-aircraft *Schwarm* fighter formation evolved from the earlier three-aircraft *Kette* used by pilots of the *Legion Condor* during the Spanish Civil War. A four-aircraft formation was found to offer greater in-flight cohesion and tactical flexibility. The *Schwarm* comprised two pairs – *Rotten* – in which one wingman, positioned behind, monitored and guarded the *Rottenführer's* (lead pilot's) course. The two *Rotten* flew in a loose line abreast formation, but with the rear *Rotte* echeloned back so that effectively the wingman concept extended by *Rotte* to the whole *Schwarm*, and resulted in a 'finger-four' formation, broadly resembling the fingers of an outstretched hand.

Generally, it was found that the best distance between aircraft was around 180–200m. As the war progressed and different mission types ensued, so the optimum spacing between aircraft could change. For example, missions in Defence of the Reich would see tighter formation flying to bring together greater firepower in an attempt to overwhelm the massed defences of enemy bomber formations. Larger formations would, in turn, be comprised of several *Schwärme*, with a lead *Schwarm* flying immediately ahead of other *Schwarm* positioned on either side, the one to the right staggered slightly further back.

autumn of 1944, Fw 190D-9-equipped III./JG 54 would practice *Schwarm* formation flying throughout the day, making up to four such flights, each lasting around an hour.

For the kind of large-scale combat missions involving 30–60 aircraft that took place from late November 1944, the D-9s of III./JG 54 would take off from their *Staffel* airfields and make for a pre-arranged rendezvous point to form into a *Gruppe*-strength formation. The *Stabsschwarm* would lead the formation, followed by two *Staffeln* staggered to port and one to starboard, with the fourth assigned to high-level cover for the whole formation.

Similarly, in the East, Heinz Radlauer of IV./JG 51 remembered:

When we were in the East with the D-9, we would often fly with a *Schwarm* of four aircraft at around 4,000–5,000m, and have another two or three aircraft a few hundred metres above and behind to create surprise if needed.

In II./JG 26, for missions flown by the whole *Gruppe*, the aircraft of 5. *Staffel* would take to the air first, heading west to east and making a turn left away from Nordhorn airfield. They would be followed by the remaining *Staffeln*, which took off to the west. Take-off would involve pairs of fighters, with 150–200m spacing between launching *Rotte*. Rendezvous with 5./JG 26 would occur over Nordhorn. *Gruppe* assembly would take place quickly, the aircraft then climbing in formation, with the *Schwärme* flying tightly in the case of poor weather until they broke through the cloud base. Werner Molg remembered, 'Above the clouds in the spring sunlight, sunglasses were needed.'

Some pilots resorted to more 'personal' methods of airborne leadership. Oberleutnant Hans Dortenmann, who was, successively, *Staffelkapitän* of 12. and 11./JG 54 (which became 14./JG 26), is acknowledged as the most successful Fw 190D-9 pilot, having claimed 18 aerial victories while flying the type. A pilot who, on occasion, would ignore orders from ground-control if he felt his impression of the situation in the air was more accurate, he noted his initiative in his diary on 20 October 1944 (Jakl, *Dortenmann*):

> In order that my pilots always know where their boss is, I order that my aircraft's tail
> is painted bright yellow. That is very colourful and can be seen for a great distance.
> I don't care if the Americans and British will take mine to be a leader's aircraft;
> I have my pride too. With my little yellow tail everything works out fine. I don't
> have to scream my head off when the novices fly after the wrong aircraft during a
> diving attack, and they save themselves a dressing down after they land.

However, despite all attempts at teaching tactical formations, rules of engagement and operational 'theory', the reality of aerial combat for piston-engined fighters over northwest Europe by late 1944 and into 1945 was that once the enemy was sighted and encountered, formations would quickly break up into short, sharp, wild dogfights involving small or large numbers of aircraft. These were often fought at close range, and usually were over in seconds. The high-speed confusion of such a melee often proved fatal to young, less experienced pilots on both sides.

In the West, in its mission of 27 December 1944, for example, the whole of III./JG 54 at Varrelbusch was assigned to provide airfield cover for the Ar 234 jet bombers of *Kampfgeschwader* 76's 9. *Staffel* at Münster-Handorf. The D-9s took off shortly after midday, with *Staffel* following *Staffel*. Turning over Varrelbusch, the *Gruppe* headed south in a climb, with the *Stabsschwarm* leading, followed by 9., 11. and 12. *Staffeln* at staggered heights to port and starboard, while 10. *Staffel*, led by 20-victory ace Leutnant Peter Crump, flew top cover.

Over the Münster area, the D-9s ran into eight Tempest Vs from No 486 Sqn undertaking an armed reconnaissance mission to the Paderborn area. On being alerted to the presence of the Tempest Vs by ground control, the *Gruppenkommandeur*, Hauptmann Weiss, ordered the large German formation to alter course from the southwest to the northeast. This split the lower *Staffeln* from Crump's *Staffel* and isolated it. Worse, as Crump ordered his pilots to reverse, they lost contact, dispersed and lagged behind the rest of the *Gruppe*.

A fast-weaving dogfight broke out and three D-9s were shot down. Crump managed to turn tightly to position himself onto the tail of a Tempest V that was in turn pursuing another D-9 in his *Schwarm*. He registered strikes on the British fighter, forcing its pilot, Flg Off Bevan Hall, to bail out of his stricken machine as it fell away in a vertical dive. The spiralling Tempest V careered into the parachute of Oberleutnant Paul Breger from 10./JG 54 as he floated towards the ground after bailing out, having been attacked by the RAF fighters. Breger plummeted downwards with his parachute in flames.

EARLY AFTERNOON, 27 DECEMBER 1944

OVERHEAD MÜNSTER-HANDORF AIRFIELD

1   A formation of eight Tempest Vs of No 486 Sqn is on an armed reconnaissance to the Paderborn area, passing near Münster-Handorf airfield at an altitude of 3,000m. The Tempest Vs are flying in two sections of four aircraft.

2   A *Gruppe*-sized formation of 60+ Fw 190D-9s from III./JG 54 is on a large-scale airfield protection flight for returning Ar 234 jet bombers of 9./KG 76. The D-9s are in a staggered formation at between 2,000–3,000m, led by the *Stabsschwarm*. To the left and right of the *Stab* are, 9., 11. and 12. *Staffeln*, while flying top cover are the 12 Focke-Wulfs of 10. *Staffel*, led by Leutnant Peter Crump.

3   When the German formation spots the Tempest Vs, its commander, Hauptmann Robert Weiss, orders it to alter course from the southwest to the northeast. This splits the lower *Staffeln* from Crump's *Staffel* and isolates it. Worse, as Crump orders his pilots to reverse, they lose contact, disperse and lag behind the rest of the *Gruppe*.

4   The four Tempest Vs of Green section climb to attack the high-cover Fw 190D-9s of 10./JG 54 at 4,200m, while those of Red section take on the main force. A large fighter-versus-fighter dogfight ensues. Green section climbs into the scattered German *Staffel*, and one Fw 190 blows up and another disintegrates and falls downwards.

5   Despite losing two fighters from his *Staffel*, Crump manages to turn tightly to position himself on the tail of a Tempest V, which itself is in pursuit of another D-9 from his *Schwarm*. The No 486 Sqn fighter is flown by Flg Off Bevan Hall, who attempts to come to the assistance of Flg Off Jack Stafford.

6   Crump manages to hit Hall's Tempest V and forces him to bail out of his burning aircraft, which rolls onto its back and enters a vertical dive.

7   The Tempest V then flies into the parachute of Oberleutnant Paul Breger from 10./JG 54 as he floats down, having bailed out following Green section's initial attack. The British fighter crashes into the ground on the road between Handorf and Dorbaum, exploding on impact. Breger plummets to earth with his parachute in flames, and Hall is later found dead as well. Crump is credited with the destruction of Hall's and Stafford's Tempest Vs for his 21st and 22nd victories, although Stafford manages to nurse his damaged fighter back to No 486 Sqn's Volkel airfield.

FOLLOWING PAGES

One German pilot wrote in his diary following the encounter, 'I just escaped from a wild dogfight with my skin. Our formation disintegrated completely, no trace of an "air battle", just wild confusion'. Another mentioned in a letter home, 'I must praise my machine.'

The net result was that No 486 Sqn had shot down five Fw 190D-9s and damaged a sixth for the loss of Flg Off Bevan Hall and his Tempest V. The men of the mauled 10./JG 54 were so affected by their experience that 'Bazzi' Weiss decided to rest them for a few days.

On 5 April 1945, the Fw 190D-9s of all three still operational *Gruppen* of JG 26 were in action on armed reconnaissance, strafing or bombing missions. Around 20 D-9s of IV. *Gruppe* were despatched from Varrelbusch, led by the *Kommandeur*, Major Rudolf Klemm, to strafe enemy targets in the area between Rheine and Hengelo. As the 'Doras' flew southwest towards the battlefront at around midday, they encountered a formation of Spitfire XIVs from the Royal Canadian Air Force's No 402 Sqn. The Allied fighters were led by Flt Lt E. R. Burrows, out on patrol over the Lingen area. Northeast of that town, the two groups of aircraft headed straight for each other.

In the heat of battle, the Fw 190D-9s were mistaken for Bf 109s – a common occurrence. Flt Lt W. F. Peck of Red Section recorded three separate combats in this one encounter:

FIRST COMBAT
I was flying Red 5 on a patrol of the Lingen area when I sighted and reported 12-plus e/a flying towards us on a westerly course. We broke into them and I attacked a Me 109, giving him a 3-second burst from 4/500 yds, 20° port deflection. I saw strikes on the fuselage, the e/a then pulled up into cloud and disappeared.

An Me 262 is caught at low level by the gun camera of a pursuing USAAF fighter as its pilot reduces speed and attempts to land. This was the moment that the German jets were at their most vulnerable, and so the Fw 190D-9 *Gruppen* were brought in to provide airfield cover for Me 262s and Ar 234s during take-offs and landings. (Author)

This may have been the D-9 of Leutnant Hans Prager, *Staffelkapitän* of 14./JG 26, whose wingman, Oberfähnrich Heinz Birkner, had alerted the Spitfires' presence to his comrades. This prompted the more experienced Prager to manoeuvre his Focke-Wulf into a 'brutal climbing left turn', which Birkner tried to follow. A second later, Peck attacked again:

SECOND COMBAT

I attacked the second 109, giving a 1- to 2-second burst from 300 yds, 30° port, seeing strikes on port wing roots. He started down in a gentle spiral, trailing black smoke. At this time I had to break sharply to avoid a long-nosed 190 who attacked from above.

This 'long-nosed 190' may have been Prager, who managed to get behind a Spitfire and open fire at close range, but Peck did not go down. In fact, he struck again:

THIRD COMBAT

I engaged a Fw 190 firing a ¾-second burst from 150/200 yds, 10/15° deflection port. Bits of his starboard wing flew off, he flicked and went straight down. The e/a was at 1,500ft when the flick occurred. I then noticed 3 more Fw 190s to port and turned into them, selecting the No. 3 to attack. We half-rolled right down to the deck, and I caught up to him on the deck after covering about 5 miles. I closed in to 100 yards but had no ammo left. I broke off and re-joined the formation.

Peck's victim in his third combat was most likely Oberfähnrich Günter Schitkowsky, a replacement pilot who had only recently joined 13./JG 26. His Fw 190D-9 was seen by Flt Lt Burrows 'blazing on the ground some 8 miles NNE of Lingen', which broadly ties in with the location of Huden, where Schitkowsky's aircraft was found in 1950. The *Gruppe* also lost Unteroffizier Kurt Söder of 15. *Staffel*, another replacement. Prager and Feldwebel Hermann Sinz of 15./JG 26 each claimed a Spitfire, but No 402 Sqn lost no aircraft.

As previously noted, a prime mission for the Fw 190D-9 was providing airfield cover for the Luftwaffe's Me 262 and Ar 234 jet units. The jets themselves may have represented the zenith in aircraft technology, but they were not without weaknesses. Perhaps most dangerous of all were the vulnerable moments when an Me 262 or Ar 234 prepared to take off, or when they approached for landing, as greater lengths of time and distance were required than for conventional fighter aircraft. The Me 262 also needed a longer period of time to start its engines, and this would frequently have to be done in the open, thus exposing the aircraft to the very real threat of attack from Allied fighters.

From mid-October 1944 at Achmer and Hesepe, 9. and 12./JG 54 began to prepare for this role, commencing with training missions intended to familiarise pilots with the surrounding landscape, the airfield layout and locations of the airfield Flak defences. Protection flights would be carried out as a defensive circle at 400m at the time the jets were taking off, with each aircraft covering the machine in front of it, thus making attack by enemy fighters much harder.

On 2 November 1944, for example, the Fw 190D-9s of 12./JG 54 took off in the early afternoon for Achmer, home of the Me 262 interceptor

Fw 190D-9 Wk-Nr. 210240 'Red 13' of JV 44 was photographed at Ainring with Bf 109Gs of II./JG 52. In English, the motif applied to the side read 'In he goes even though both of us will cry!' (Author's Collection)

evaluation unit *Kommando Nowotny*. Upon arriving in the vicinity of the base, the Focke-Wulf pilots formed into a defensive circle and waited in the sky over the airfield. After a delayed start, the jets carried out their mission against USAAF bombers and returned, with the D-9s having remained over the airfield throughout the time the Me 262s were aloft. The 12. *Staffel* undertook a similar mission later that afternoon, and again there was no contact made with the enemy.

Six days later, 'Doras' of 9. and 12./JG 54 were circling over Hesepe, again covering for *Kommando Nowotny*. A small number of the *Kommando's* Me 262s had gone up to attack USAAF bombers returning to England after attacking the synthetic fuel plant at Leuna-Merseburg and the marshalling yards at Rheine. One of the jet pilots, Leutnant Franz Schall, shot down what he thought was a pair of P-51s, but they were actually P-47s. One of the fighters was flown by Lt Charles C. McKelvy of the 359th FS/365th FG, which had been escorting bombers of the 1st Bomb Division (BD) targeting Leuna-Merseburg.

With his fighter badly damaged by fire from Schall's Me 262, McKelvy became separated from his squadron and was subsequently spotted by Leutnant Hans Prager of 9./JG 54. Prager pursued the Thunderbolt as it headed south at 1,200m and eventually closed in to open fire as it neared Achmer airfield. Under attack, the American fighter force-landed 500m south of the airfield.

Another Me 262 unit to use the Fw 190D-9 to provide airfield cover was *Jagdverband* (JV) 44, which had been established in February 1945 under the command of the former *General der Jagdflieger*, Generalleutnant Adolf Galland. He had established JV 44 as a unit of 'exiled' aces who had fallen foul of Göring, augmented by former officer and NCO instructor pilots, at Brandenburg-Briest to 'prove' to the higher authorities that the Me 262 was an effective jet fighter. This small unit had moved south to Munich-Riem at the end of March, from where it carried out sporadic, small-scale operations, mainly against US tactical bombers over southern Germany and Austria.

Walter Krupinski, who had commanded D-9-equipped III./JG 26 prior to joining JV 44, recalled:

The problem for us was that every time we took off and landed in the Me 262, there were enemy fighter aircraft active either very near to us or actually over the field.

The front was just on the other side of Munich, and as a result of this situation was born the idea to form a special unit to protect us. You couldn't do much with an Me 262 on a landing pass; you had very low speed, and if you tried to accelerate, you needed too much time. It was a time when we were vulnerable. So came the idea to use the Fw 190D-9s.

A small number of such machines was assembled under the command of Knight's Cross-holder and 104-victory ace Leutnant Heinz Sachsenberg. The most reliable documentary evidence indicates that five Fw 190Ds were attached to JV 44 in what was the unit's *Platzschutzschwarm* (Airfield Defence Flight), although it cannot be ruled out that there were more. Three of the Focke-Wulfs were D-9s, while two were rarer D-11 models.

Walter Krupinski remembered:

They were based very near to us – parked on the northern edge of the airfield and hidden in trees. They came out when we were due to start, and we felt very safe when we were getting airborne or landing knowing they were there. It was a good idea of Galland's to have those Focke-Wulfs there.

Within a short period of time, so it would seem, the 'Doras' of the *Platzschutzschwarm* were brought up to readiness and flew their first covering flights. By the evening of 23 April, JV 44 reported five Fw 190Ds on strength, but only two aircraft were serviceable.

Four veteran pilots of JV 44's *Platzschutzschwarm* gather for a photograph in front of one of their Fw 190D-9s at Ainring in May 1945. They are, from left to right, Leutnant Karl-Heinz Hofmann, Leutnant Heinz Sachsenberg, Hauptmann Waldemar Wubke and Oberleutnant Klaus Faber. Note the striped underside of the Focke-Wulf (in red and white), which was intended as a visual recognition aid. (Author's Collection)

Tactics were simple – flights were to be undertaken in two-aircraft *Rotte* up to an altitude of 460m, all the while keeping eyes on both the Me 262s taking off or landing and the surrounding skies over Riem for enemy fighters. Sachsenberg also gave strict orders that his pilots were neither to break off from their 'chained dog' mission or to attempt to fly alongside the jets.

One major problem was that in order to give the Me 262s a clear landing approach, the Focke-Wulfs had to land before the jets returned from a sortie, thus nullifying any offer of protection. Ground control would give them clearance to land, but there was no radio contact between the Me 262s and the Fw 190s. Feldwebel Bodo Dirschauer, formerly with JG 6 and assigned at some point to JV 44, apparently flew 12 such protection flights over Riem, including three on one day in mid-April. Adolf Galland recalled:

> The Americans were constantly observing our airfields and they attacked anybody who came out or who tried to get in, especially at Munich-Riem once they knew we were there. We lost some of our men that way. Sachsenberg was a good pilot and we felt safer when his aircraft were in the air. They surrounded the airfield – not in any formation – but usually just in pairs. We tried to get them into the air just as we took off, and also when we came in to land, but often it didn't work because conditions were becoming impossible both on the airfield and in the air. Once up, they escorted us around the airfield – once the Me 262s' undercarriages were up and they had climbed, it was time for the Focke-Wulfs to come back.

As a measure intended to offer clear identification of its Fw 190D-9s by both the Me 262 pilots and the wary Flak defences at Riem, JV 44 introduced a unique recognition feature through the application of red paint with unevenly spaced white stripes on the undersides of its D-9s.

On at least one occasion, it is known that the Focke-Wulfs engaged P-47s in combat over Riem while flying a cover sortie for the Me 262s.

Fw 190D-9 Wk-Nr. 600?69 'Red 3' of JV 44 at Ainring in May 1945, with its distinctively painted red and white striped underside. The front of the spinner was painted in yellow, with the rear section in black. This aircraft is believed to have been flown by 14-victory ace Hauptmann Waldemar Wübke, who had joined JV 44 in mid-April 1945 from II./JG 101, where he had served as *Kommandeur*. The port side of his aircraft carried the sardonic inscription 'On Orders of the Reich Railways'. (Author)

CHAPTER 6
COMBAT

Throughout the autumn of 1944, following its debut with III./JG 54, the Fw 190D-9 was steadily delivered to more fighter *Gruppen*, and by the end of the year it was in service with III./JG 54, I. and III./JG 2 and I. and II./JG 26. For example, I./JG 2 received 54 'Doras' in December, while III. *Gruppe* took on 53.

Leutnant Karl-Heinz Ossenkop of I./JG 26 was one of the first pilots in his *Geschwader* to fly the Fw 190D-9. In terms of manoeuvrability against the Tempest V, Ossenkop felt that the 'Dora' had the edge in the climb and in turns, that it was comparable or perhaps less able in level flight, depending on the individual machine, but that it had a lower diving speed, which was where the MW 50 boost could be a valuable aid. However, in a dive, the Tempest was better. It was a similar situation when fighting the big American P-47 Thunderbolt, in comparison to which Ossenkop believed the D-9 was superior in the turn and the climb, equal at level speed but lacking severely in diving speed. 'We were hopelessly inferior in a dive', he noted. 'Never try to dive away from a Thunderbolt.'

Against the P-51D, the aircraft were on a par in most respects, but again the Mustang had the edge in a dive.

Ossenkop joined 2./JG 26 in August 1944, fresh from operational flight training with JG 103. He had been with his *Gruppe* for less than two weeks when he first encountered USAAF P-51s. Ossenkop was typical of many young Luftwaffe fighter pilots who had to absorb their initial operational experience in extremely unfavourable conditions as they fought to defend the skies over northwest Europe and cover the German ground forces' inexorable retreat eastwards out of France. Outnumbered, with frequent changes of base, it was a demoralising period for many, with little reason for hope or cheer.

Shortly after his arrival with his *Staffel*, Ossenkop was advised starkly by an experienced Knight's Cross-holder to whom he was detailed to fly as

Leutnant Karl-Heinz Ossenkop of I./JG 26 took a balanced view of the Fw 190D-9 as a combat aircraft, recognising both its strong points and shortcomings. He flew the D-9 in Operation *Bodenplatte*, during which his aircraft was damaged by another 'Dora', and claimed his first victory flying the type on 14 January 1945. (Dietmar Hermann Collection)

wingman that he should stick with his leader, secure his rear and not even think about achieving any aerial success for six weeks. Gaining experience was the key to staying alive, not glory. Sensibly, Ossenkop listened.

The war ground on, but one glimmer of encouragement was the arrival in December 1944 of the Fw 190D-9. Ossenkop's *Gruppe* had to familiarise itself with, and train up on, the new fighter while still remaining operational. He remembered (Caldwell, *JG 26 War Diary*, pg 420–421):

> The Fw 190D-9 was quickly adopted by the pilots, after some initial reservations. They felt it was equal to or better than the equipment of the opposition. Its serviceability was not so good, owing to the circumstances. I felt that aircraft built at Sorau had the best fit and finish. I hit 600km/h in my 'own' aircraft, 'Black 8', with full power and MW 50, clean, 20–30m above the ground.
>
> Compared with the Fw 190A-8, the 'Dora-9': 1) with 40–50 more horsepower had a greater level speed, climb rate and ceiling; 2) had much better visibility to the rear, owing to its bubble canopy; 3) was much quieter – the Jumo 213A vibrated much less than the BMW 801; 4) handled better in steep climbs and turning, probably because of its greater shaft horsepower at full throttle; 5) had less torque effect on take-off or landing; and 6) had greater endurance.

All three *Gruppen* of JG 26 supported the German offensive in the Ardennes in December. II. *Gruppe* took on no fewer than 74 D-9s in mid-December, and enjoyed the benefit of training away from the front. They returned, to Nordhorn-Klausheide, for operations.

Oberleutnant Hans Hartigs had been with II./JG 26 since July 1943, but while returning from a mission over France on 15 August 1944 he had been bounced by P-47s. In bailing out, he collided with his Fw 190's tail

Groundcrew pose for a photograph with an Fw 190D-9 of 6./JG 301 possibly at Sachau, near Gardelegen, in December 1944. The inscription *Glykol!*, clearly visible on the cowling, has been applied to remind mechanics of the need to use coolant. The barrel of the MG 151/20E cannon in the port wing root is clearly visible, and the aircraft is fitted with the more common 300-litre drop tank. (EN Archive)

fin and suffered a broken pelvis, jaw and ribs and was hospitalised until October. After a subsequent period of leave, and assignment as commander of a Flak battery, Hartigs was declared fit for flying and managed to get re-posted back to 4./JG 26.

He claimed a P-47 probably destroyed over the Western Front on Christmas Day 1944 when Fw 190s from all three of JG 26's *Gruppen* scoured the Dinant area searching for enemy fighter-bombers and tactical medium bombers. Hartigs was one of five 'Dora' pilots from his *Gruppe* in action that day when they found a large formation of American fighters and bombers. He dove on the enemy aircraft from head-on, briefly opening fire and then climbing rapidly away in a hit-and-run style attack.

Taking on a P-47 was one thing, but the P-51 was another matter entirely, as Hartigs explained to a fellow PoW when in Allied captivity:

> Even an outstanding pilot can't get away properly from a Mustang by banking in that '190'; it's out of the question. I tried it. *It's out of the question.*

On the morning of 26 December, with troops from Lt Gen George S. Patton's Third Army closing on the besieged Belgian town of Bastogne, Hartigs led 15 Fw 190D-9s from I./JG 26 on what was intended as a ground-controlled patrol over the Ardennes, watching out for enemy aircraft harassing German ground forces. However, with the failure of his FuG 16ZY transceiver, Hartigs ordered the 'Doras' to proceed on the basis of a *freie Jagd* ('free hunt'), as he had no confidence that any of the other pilots with him could assume leadership of the formation. Hartigs flew on and eventually reached the positions of the 12. SS Panzer-Division *'Hitlerjugend'* (HJ). He recounts (Eriksson, *Alarmstart*, pg 214–215):

> In December 1944 I flew various missions from Fürstenau against the four-engined bombers and against American and English fighters as *Staffelführer* and *Gruppenführer*. On 26 December I had the instruction to take the *Gruppe* over the leading elements of the Hitler Youth (*HJ*) Division in the Ardennes – at low level – to counter the enemy fighter-bomber attacks on them. In this area [the southern tip of Belgium, near Charleroi], with 14 of my 16 new aircraft – it had been very cold overnight and the mechanics had struggled to start the new Fw *'Langnase'* aircraft, as they did not have enough experience of them yet, and many would not start; I could not keep circling over the base waiting for them due to fuel with time limitations – we found the leading elements of the *HJ* division. The tanks were abandoned and partly dug in. Apparently, their supplies of fuel and ammunition had not reached them.
>
> At that time, for such missions, there was a standing order forbidding a return without engaging the enemy, so I climbed from low-level in the direction of Luxembourg and into the sun, towards the south. Unfortunately, soon after take-off, my radio had failed and I could not communicate with my men. They could not hear me either, as I soon established by hand signals with my wingman.

While still climbing I saw Allied fighters and counted about 60 'Indians'. A fighter group climbing above me led by Maj Emmeroy attacked me in the precise moment that I made a half-turn away to attack four Thunderbolts below me. I shot down a Thunderbolt, and in the same moment my aircraft burst into flames. Emmeroy had shot me down. I bailed out at c. 5,000m and landed in a very high pine tree in dense forest. My parachute caught in the top of one of the trees and, after some swinging and struggling, I got loose from my harness and slid down the very thick trunk like a monkey. That was the end of my war experiences, the beginning of my life as a PoW and then, later sadly, as a Russian captive!

Hans Hartigs had claimed six victories in total.

On 1 January 1945, Generalmajor Dietrich Peltz, commander of II. *Jagdkorps*, oversaw Operation *Bodenplatte*, a mass, low-level, ground-attack operation directed against 11 key Allied fighter airfields in Belgium, the Netherlands and northeastern France. Peltz reasoned that the best way in which to offer support to the armoured thrust in the Ardennes was to neutralise Allied tactical air power where it was at its most vulnerable – on the ground. By using the element of surprise, Peltz had logically concluded that as an alternative to the costly dogfights against numerically superior and skilled enemy fighter pilots over the front, such an attack would incur minimum casualties and consume less fuel.

Originally intended to coincide with the launch of the Ardennes counteroffensive (codenamed *Unternehmen Wacht am Rhein* – 'Operation Watch on the Rhine' – by the Germans), the weather frustrated the plan and the operation was deferred, despite the commencement of the ground counteroffensive on 16 December. Thus, at first light on New Year's morning, under complete radio silence, fighters from 33 *Gruppen* left their airfields and headed in tight formation across the snow-covered landscape towards the Allied lines. Included in the strike force were the Fw 190D-9-equipped *Stab*, I. and III./JG 2, which had been tasked with targeting St. Trond, and *Stab*, I. and II./JG 26 and III./JG 54, attacking Brussels-Evere and Grimbergen.

Exhaust clouds the chill air beneath an Fw 190D-9 of 3./JG 26 as it emerges from the treeline at a snow-covered Fürstenau airfield in the winter of 1944–45. A second D-9 waits with its engine running in the trees to the right. As the view ahead for the pilot when on the ground was very restricted, the groundcrew would guide him with hand signals when taxiing. (EN Archive)

Altogether, nearly 300 Allied aircraft were destroyed as a result of *Bodenplatte*, of which some 145 were single-engined fighters. A further 180 Allied aircraft were damaged in the attack and 185 personnel killed or wounded. *Bodenplatte* was, without doubt, an unexpected and painful blow for the Allies, but the effect on Allied tactical operations would be negligible. In total, 143 German pilots were killed or reported missing, including three *Geschwaderkommodore*, five *Gruppenkommandeure* and 14 *Staffelkapitäne*, with a further 21 pilots wounded and 70 taken prisoner.

The aircraft of Feldwebel Werner Hohenberg of the *Stabsschwarm* of I./JG 2 arouses the interest of two US Army officers as it lies wrecked in snowy countryside near the village of Dorff, in southeastern Germany, following its crash-landing during Operation *Bodenplatte* on 1 January 1945. Hohenberg's 'Dora', Wk-Nr. 210194, had been hit by fire from American antiaircraft artillery while making a low-level pass over the airfield at St. Trond. The fighter carries the chevron and bars of a *Stab* aircraft, as well as the yellow-white-yellow Reich defence identification band markings forward of the tailplane that were unique to JG 2. (EN Archive)

JG 2 made best endeavours to reach St. Trond, but its attack was a total failure. The *Geschwader* suffered particularly heavy losses in the process from American anti-aircraft fire as they flew over the Ardennes battle area. A few Focke-Wulfs reached the target, including a small number of D-9s fitted with underwing 21cm mortars, but their effect was minimal.

Things were little better in the strikes on Brussels-Evere and Grimbergen by JG 26 and JG 54. II./JG 26 did operate according to plan and it did find and attack its target at Brussels-Evere, claiming the destruction of 20 B-17s and B-24s, 24 twin-engined aircraft and 60 fighters, whereas Allied losses on the ground are reported as 45. Certainly 15 Spitfires were destroyed or damaged, as well as several Ansons, Austers and Dakotas, including those belonging to the commander of the 2nd TAF! But JG 26 suffered no fewer than 22 Fw 190D-9s destroyed or damaged during *Bodenplatte*, most of them falling to 'friendly' Flak.

Leutnant Karl-Heinz Ossenkop of I./JG 26 had suffered severe damage to his aircraft while attacking Grimbergen when its rudder and part of the starboard horizontal stabiliser were removed by the propeller of another D-9, but he managed to make it to Twenthe, where he made an emergency landing.

Ossenkop subsequently claimed his first aerial victory flying the Fw 190D-9 when, in the late afternoon of 14 January 1945, he was included in a patrol from Fürstenau led by his *Gruppenkommandeur*, Major Karl Borris, to the Me 262 jet bomber airfields in the Rheine-Hopsten area. No fewer than 31 Fw 190D-9s were involved, although three machines dropped out. The remaining 28 Focke-Wulfs subsequently encountered a formation of 24 Spitfire IXs from Nos 331 and 332 (Norwegian) Sqns from Woensdrecht, led by Maj Martin Gran from the former squadron, which happened to be conducting a sweep of Rheine, Achmer and Plantlünne airfields.

Like the D-9s of I./JG 26, three Spitfires of No 331 Sqn developed mechanical problems and were forced to abort, having had to return to base with a fourth fighter as an escort. The remaining eight aircraft first encountered Bf 109s, followed shortly thereafter by the 'Doras' of JG 26 midway between Rheine and Osnabrück to the west. As the two groups of aircraft met, the skies over northern Westphalia began to fill with the drone and chatter of aerial dogfights. Leading Blue Section of No 331 Sqn was Capt H. Grundt-Spang in a Spitfire IXB. His Combat Report from the action that ensued read as follows:

> The Squadron was flying on a Westerly course towards the Rheine area when I noticed about 20 enemy aircraft crossing underneath us, going South. I was Blue 1, and as soon as I had reported them the whole squadron attacked. The Huns saw us break into our attack and a general dogfight followed. I got my sight on a long-nosed Fw 190 at a distance of about 200 yards, approximately 30 degrees deflection, and after a two-second burst, the enemy aircraft was hit in the engine and started to burn. He went down in a 20-degree dive and crashed in a wood about a mile to the East. This was witnessed by 2/Ltn Roald.

Fully aware of the danger posed by so many Spitfire IXs, Major Borris ordered his pilots to form a wide defensive Lufbery circle over the town of Ibbenbüren. Indeed, just to the south of where Grundt-Spang had observed his victim crash:

> I noticed about 30 Fw 190s orbiting in a defensive circle on the deck. Another formation of enemy aircraft also totalling about 30 aircraft came from the south and joined the defensive circle, which was complete and tight. I informed the squadron, and while waiting, I carried out four attacks, diving down from 8,000 to 1,000ft, squirting at one each time and pulling up very fast. The only result I was able to notice was a cannon hit on one aircraft.

As the Focke-Wulfs commenced their second full turn, Ossenkop recalled another lone Spitfire breaking into the circle. 'I thought the man was very bold or crazy, as he flew right into my gunsight!' This was probably Spitfire IX PT945 FN-Z, flown by 2Lt John Ditlev-Simonsen also of No 331 Sqn. According to the unit's Operations Record Book (ORB), he had just shot down a Focke-Wulf.

Ossenkop opened fire on Ditlev-Simonsen from a range of 200m as the Spitfire banked sharply to the right. In order to gain on his quarry in the dive, Ossenkop engaged his MW 50 boost and the distance between the two fighters closed. At a range of 80m, Ossenkop fired again and then flew past his quarry, catching sight of the Spitfire as it fell in the direction of the snow-covered fields trailing smoke, before exploding in flames when it hit the ground. Ditlev-Simonsen's comrades also witnessed the crash. The squadron diarist noted:

Unfortunately, 2Lt Ditlev-Simonsen, being unable to pull up after chasing a Fw 190 which he shot down, was seen to crash into the ground.

It was perhaps fortunate that Ossenkop had chased Ditlev-Simonsen in a dive, for it was his opinion that set against the Spitfire IX, the D-9 had greater overall speeds, but was unable to better the British fighter in either a horizontal turn or a steep climbing turn – manoeuvres often needed in aerial combat.

JG 26 listed three D-9 casualties, all from 1. *Staffel*, as a result of the engagement with the Norwegians. The Focke-Wulf flown by Unteroffizier Karl Russ was reported as having collided with a Spitfire, with both aircraft crashing in flames. Major Borris, a JG 26 veteran who had served with the *Geschwader* since December 1939, and who had been awarded the Knight's Cross on 25 November 1944 in recognition of his then 41 victories, also claimed a Spitfire shot down over Ibbenbüren. Ditlev-Simonsen was No 331 Sqn's only loss, although No 332 Sqn reported two of its pilots, Lt R. G. Hassel and Sgt T. Syversen, missing after the action, so it is possible one of these two pilots was shot down by Borris and the other may have collided with Russ. The Spitfire would be Borris' 43rd, and final, victory.

The four Spitfires comprising Yellow Section of No 332 Sqn had also spotted enemy aircraft 'on the deck' between Rheine and Osnabrück and went down to attack. Flying as 'Yellow 4' was 2Lt O. Wagtskjold:

I was flying at 1,000ft when I saw 20+ Fw 190s doing a right hand circuit 500ft below. I called up my No. 3 and reported them. Then I picked one out of the bunch and got on his tail. Opened fire at about 200–300 yards and saw strikes,

SPITFIRE DOWN

On 14 January 1945, Leutnant Karl-Heinz Ossenkop of I./JG 26 puts his Fw 190D-9 'Black 8' into a sharp right turn, applying full boost, and breaking away from the defensive Lufbery circle ordered earlier by his *Gruppenkommandeur*, Major Karl Borris, as he pursues a Spitfire IX of No 331 (Norwegian) Sqn over Ibbenbüren. The 'Doras' of I./JG 26 had taken off from their base at Fürstenau, 30km to the north, to provide airfield cover to the Me 262s of I./KG 51 at Rheine, but had encountered a formation of 24 Spitfire IXs to the east of the jet base.

Opening fire on an enemy machine from a distance of 200m, Ossenkop doggedly remained on the Spitfire's tail as it attempted to evade the chase by diving to the right. Eventually, the D-9 pilot closed to within 80m of his quarry and opened fire again, flying past and over the

Spitfire as it disappeared beneath the cowling of the Focke-Wulf, streaming white smoke. It soon rolled onto its back and crashed into snow-covered ground near the confluence of the Dortmund-Ems and Mittelland canals. No 331 Sqn listed Spitfire IX PT945 FN-Z of 2Lt John Ditlev-Simonsen as missing, and he may have been Ossenkop's victim.

Karl-Heinz Ossenkop had entered the Luftwaffe in 1942, and after completion of his initial training, he volunteered for fighter operations and was posted to JG 103 in May 1944 for operational training on the Fw 190. On 23 August 1944 he was assigned to 2./JG 26. The Spitfire on 14 January was Ossenkop's first victory, and he would score another, over a Tempest V, while flying an Fw 190D-9 on 12 April 1945.

FOLLOWING PAGES

Exhaust-blackened Fw 190D-9 Wk-Nr. 211934 was one of three 'Doras' of II./JG 6 to land at Fürth on 8 May 1945, where their pilots surrendered to local USAAF forces. The fighter's markings ('< • + –') clearly indicate a II. *Gruppe Stab* aircraft assigned to the Technical Officer. (EN Archive)

several of them in the cowling and the enemy aircraft was smoking. It did a half roll and flicked onto the deck. I pulled away as I saw three Fw 190s in the mirror on my tail. When I next looked down I saw smoke and fire from the aircraft which had crashed.

Grundt-Spang's and Wagtskjold's victims were probably Unteroffiziere Kurt Ullerich and Friedrich Worster. Ullerich managed to bail out, but was killed when his parachute failed to open. His D-9 crashed at Lengerich. Worster, whose aircraft came down northeast of Ibbenbüren, also bailed out, suffering injuries in the process.

During the encounter, the D-9 formation was widely scattered, with six 'Doras' being chased by Spitfires south as far as Dortmund, where they managed to land with their fuel almost expended. Borris returned to Fürstenau with just 12 aircraft.

Over the coming weeks Allied fighters virtually ruled the skies over Germany, and even though the Luftwaffe could still – sporadically – hit back, for RAF and USAAF fighter pilots, the air war was fast becoming a game of 'cat and mouse'. But it was still a tough, deadly game nevertheless.

On 7 March, one encounter served to indicate how marginal and demanding combats between another British fighter, the Tempest V, and the Fw 190D-9 were, and how a single 'Dora' could evade even the fastest Allied piston-engined fighters. At 1400 hrs, eight Tempest Vs from No 3 Sqn led by Flt Lt B. C. McKenzie, together with other Tempest Vs from No 56 Sqn, took off from Volkel on a wing sweep of the Rheine-Bielefeld area.

At Plantlünne orders were received from *Luftwaffenkommando West* for III./JG 26 to carry out a full-strength *freie Jagd* to Enschede. Because of the unavailability of more senior formation leaders, the mission was to be led by Oberfeldwebel Willi Zester of 9. *Staffel*, who, although an experienced pilot, had never previously led a formation. Eventually, after waiting at cockpit readiness for some time, 17 Fw 190D-9s took off from Plantlünne, climbed to 3,000m and flew directly to Enschede, where they found the skies to be active with Spitfires and Typhoons. Turning east towards Rheine, the Focke-Wulfs were now on a 'collision course' with the Tempest Vs.

Flying as 'Red 3' within the No 3 Sqn formation was Flg Off Vasilios Vassiliades, an accomplished Greek pilot from the island of Chios serving in the RAF. By 7 March he had been credited with ten enemy aircraft shot down (two of them shared), one probable, one damaged and one ground victory. Shortly after 1530 hrs, Vassiliades was flying northwest, some 8km northeast of Enschede, when his formation was jumped by five Bf 109s out of the winter sun. Vassiliades broke into the Messerschmitts but was unable to gain a position on any of the assailants as they dived towards the ground. He pulled out and away, climbing to 8,000ft, and as he did so he caught sight of 'a long-nosed Fw 190 approx. 1,000 ft above flying SE'.

This was Unteroffizier Karl-Georg Genth of 12./JG 26 who was flying in Wk-Nr. 500118 'Yellow 15' as wingman to Oberfeldwebel Zester. Genth remembered (Caldwell, *Top Guns*, pg 359):

> We quickly reached the battle zone at an altitude of 3,000m. We were to determine the amount of enemy activity around Enschede. Typhoons were busy attacking motor convoys. Spitfires could be seen banking to one side, but they did not spot our formation. Then we saw several flights of Tempests below us. This was very dangerous, as our best combat altitude, at which the Fw 190D-9 was superior to the Tempest, began at 5,000m. Thus it probably happened that the Tempest flights were able to approach our formation without being noticed, using their superb rate of climb at 3,000m.

TOP In this photograph of Fw 190D-9 Wk-Nr. 211934 of II./JG 6, its later-style, raised profile canopy and II. *Gruppe Stab* markings can be clearly seen. The fighter has attracted the interest of curious US servicemen at Fürth. (EN Archive)

ABOVE A US serviceman poses for a snapshot on the horizontal stabiliser of Wk-Nr. 211934 in the late spring of 1945. The aircraft's generally worn appearance and the dirt on the elevator are indicative of the operating conditions on the Eastern Front, and of the continual movement and transfers endured by German units in the final weeks of the war. (EN Archive)

Indeed, coming up from below, Vassiliades was closing in on Genth, and as he did so Zester chose that moment to bank away, leaving Genth to battle it out with the RAF fighters. He veered in the opposite direction and applied methanol injection into his 'Dora's' Jumo 213A engine to take it up to full power. The Focke-Wulf was now flying at 600km/h, but at that moment oil sprayed across Genth's windshield and blew over his port wing from what he assumed was a broken oil line. He quickly decided to make for a layer of cloud some 3km away at maximum speed. Although the Fw 190's engine continued to run smoothly, the Luftwaffe pilot knew he had only limited time in the air. Flg Off Vassiliades noted in his Combat Report how he:

> . . . began to close from line astern when the Hun spotted me and turned to port. I fired one ½ sec. burst from 250 yds, allowing 20° deflection and saw one strike on the starboard elevator. The enemy aircraft took violent evasive action, and closing

in I took several cine camera shots from ranges varying from 200 to 50 yds, line astern. As the Hun entered cloud, I fired another ½ sec. burst from 250 yds with 10° deflection but saw no results.

Reaching the 'sanctuary' of the cloud, Genth attempted a zoom climb so as to bring him into position for a head-on counter-attack on the Tempest Vs, which he knew were pursuing him, and at the very least break up their attack. This was not to be, for as Vassiliades reported:

When he [Genth] went into a second layer of cloud I turned to port, and as he emerged, turning in the same direction, I closed to 150 yds line astern and fired a ½ sec. burst, from which I saw strikes in the cockpit area. The hood was jettisoned, the pilot bailed out.

Vassiliades' pursuit of Genth had, by chance, been witnessed by another Tempest V pilot, Flt Lt L. R. G. Smith of No 80 Sqn, who had been flying as a section leader in a sweep to the Nienburg-Hannover-Hamm areas conducted by a Wing formation comprising Nos 80, 274 and 486 Sqns. He was west of the Rhine, lagging behind his formation because he had been unable to release one of his long-range drop tanks. Smith reported:

I saw another Tempest chasing an Fw 190 in an easterly direction, passing across my nose. I had managed to jettison my other tank, so entered into the chase. The enemy aircraft took violent evasive action and the Tempest, presumably that

A US serviceman stands in front of a row of four Fw 190D-9s of II./JG 6 that flew into Erfurt-Nord from eastern Germany in order to escape the Soviet advance. They are blue-coded 8. *Staffel* machines built by Focke-Wulf. The skeletal remains of hangars at Erfurt-Nord can just be seen behind the fighters. The Mimetall at this site was engaged in the license production of the Fw 190A-8, A-9 and D-9, the Ta 152 and Ta 154. (EN Archive)

Built by Mimetall at Erfurt, Fw 190D-9 Wk-Nr. 500570 'Blue 12' of 8./JG 6, which surrendered at Fürth-Atzenhof, was an oft-photographed aircraft. Visible here is the centreline ETC 504 rack for carrying either a drop tank or bomb, and note the heavy exhaust staining along the engine cowling. (EN Archive)

piloted by F/O Vassiliades, fired a short burst, from which I saw one strike on the tail unit. The enemy aircraft flew on under perfect control and the Tempest stayed on his tail for a considerable time, maintaining a range of 80 yds but did not appear to be firing.

The Hun turned to starboard, and as he presented a favourable target for me, I fired two ½ sec. bursts from 200 yds with deflection varying from 70° to 90°. I did not observe any strikes, but since the other Tempest had lost the range, I came in line astern, firing one 2½ sec. burst from 300 yds. Not being sure of F/O Vassiliades' position, I broke away quickly, thus having little time in which to see any results. The Hun went into cloud and turned to port, heading in a westerly direction. F/O Vassiliades appeared to lose contact at this point, so I called up on the R/T, giving the Hun's position, and we both resumed the chase. The enemy aircraft rapidly headed for another thin layer. I flew to starboard of the cloud and the other Tempest went to port. I saw the enemy aircraft emerge and turn to port, the cockpit hood was jettisoned and the pilot bailed out.

Indeed, as Genth came out of the cloud, he found a Tempest V waiting to strike. The RAF pilot opened fire with his 20mm Hispano Mk II cannon, and as Genth recalled:

. . . struck my wounded bird in the tail area. After a sharp blow, which I could feel through the control stick, my elevators failed. It was time to get out. I jettisoned the canopy at about 600km/h, released my harness and was sucked from the cockpit of my FW, which was now standing on its nose. I was hurled upside down along the fuselage and the fin struck my left arm so hard that it broke it, ripping the sleeve from my leather jacket. I felt only a sharp, painless blow to my upper arm. I took one last glance at the speedometer as I was preparing to leave; it read 650km/h.

Vassiliades observed Genth exit his Focke-Wulf and saw it crash and explode just 3km southeast of Enschede. Genth tumbled through the sky several times as he fell earthwards before he managed, awkwardly, to open his parachute very close to the ground.

New Yorker Sqn Ldr David 'Foob' Fairbanks claimed at least four Fw 190D-9s shot down during his 20 days in charge of No 274 Sqn in February 1945. He was eventually shot down by a 'Dora' from III./JG 26 on 28 February, spending the rest of the war as a PoW. (Tony Holmes Collection)

Judging by the phraseology used in No 3 Sqn's ORB, it had been a tough encounter. Vassiliades had 'hacked down a Fw 190 after ten minutes of hard fighting'.

Genth was not the only pilot to suffer injury when bailing out of a 'Dora'. An encounter between Fw 190D-9s and Tempest Vs on 22 February 1945 was a classic example of the aerial melee that could quickly develop between groups of aircraft, as a result of which pilots could suffer severe injuries. In the late afternoon of that day, a section of Tempest Vs of No 274 Sqn of the 2nd TAF had been detailed to carry out a strafing run to Rheine.

They were led by ranking Tempest V ace Sqn Ldr David Fairbanks, an American who had joined the RCAF in 1941, and who had previously served with both Nos 501 and 3 Sqns. Fairbanks was described by No 274 Sqn's diarist as the 'terror of Rheine' on account of the fact that he regularly visited that Luftwaffe jet base and its environs at some risk to himself, but with some success, having destroyed an Ar 234 and damaged an Me 262.

22 February also saw the Allied air forces launch Operation *Clarion*, a bombing offensive targeting German communications and transportation in the Netherlands and Germany. Strategic and tactical bombers struck bridges, railway stations, marshalling yards and road junctions. While the bombers bombed, Allied fighters operating at low-level scoured the airspace around the Luftwaffe's airfields.

Fairbanks had taken off from Volkel at 1700 hrs, and some 40 minutes later he was flying south from JG 26's airfield at Plantlünne towards Rheine when he first spotted a pair of D-9s, as he subsequently reported:

I was leading Blue Section, flying south from Plantlünne A/F to Rheine at 3,000ft, when I sighted 2 190s on my starboard side flying in the opposite direction. We broke and gave chase, but they got away into the 10/10 cloud at 4,000ft.

Once more flying east, we passed Rheine and continued on, and Blue two called out 3 190's to port who were firing at us and we broke into them. As we did so, I saw 6 or 7 more start to come our way. We turned it into a free for all and I picked one and started to close the range. As I did I saw it was a long-nosed type. He put up some good weaving and once I thought the ground flak was going to get him. He went for the deck once and did a sharp break up and to port, where I closed and fired, with the E/A below my nose. I couldn't see any strikes, and when I saw him again I was approx. 150 yds behind and at about 1,000 ft. The E/A did a half roll and I started to follow, but stopped because of his altitude. I saw the E/A head for the deck, and I could see him try to pull his nose up but he began to flutter and stall and then he went straight into the ground and blew up – my No. 2 saw the E/A blow up and burn.

Four more turned in behind me, firing – one put some tracer in front of me, so I started a steep turn and held it and out-climbed them into cloud. I did a few orbits to cool my engine, and we both went down through cloud on 270° and came out almost on Rheine A/F.

Twenty-two-year-old Unteroffizier Heinz Gehrke of 11./JG 26 was among four pilots from his *Gruppe* to take their aircraft up that afternoon from Plantlünne for an engine run. As he turned to return to base, Gehrke, flying Wk-Nr. 500096 'Yellow 1', was forced to suddenly pull up when another aircraft cut in front of him as he prepared to land. At that moment a Tempest V (thought initially by Gehrke to have been a Spitfire) chose to fly into the airspace, followed by others, and a dogfight ensued.

There is an anomaly between the JG 26 aircraft returning to 'Plantlünne' and Fairbanks reporting that the airfield he was over was 'Rheine', more than 20km away, as no Spitfire claims were made for an Fw 190D-9 at this time in this area. It is likely, therefore, that Fairbanks' engagement with the 'Doras' took place further north. Fairbanks continued:

> I saw one going in to land but kept on going around the field and met another coming head on slightly below. I broke into him and he pulled straight up for cloud. I stood on my tail too and fired from about 200 yds and about 60° off.

Gehrke's attempt to evade the Tempest Vs failed, for his fighter was hit and he quickly jettisoned his canopy. To Fairbanks it appeared as if the D-9 almost stalled:

> I saw him burst into flames at the wing roots and the cockpit, the E/A rolling over slowly and going straight down. I saw the pilot bail out at about 500 ft.

But as the Fw 190D-9 dived, Gehrke found himself caught by the airframe. After a few frantic moments, he managed to break free and his parachute blossomed. The aircraft fell away on fire until it hit the ground and exploded near Dreierwalde. Gehrke was later found by local residents near to where he had landed. They summoned a doctor and he was moved to a hospital at Lingen, where he was treated for second and third degree burns to his face and hands, shrapnel splinters to both legs and a cannon shell wound to his left foot. Fairbanks claimed two 'long-nosed' Fw 190s destroyed, taking his growing tally to ten victories.

In the hands of the right pilot, the combination of performance and experienced handling could make the Fw 190D-9 a lethal opponent, as even P-51D pilots discovered in the final weeks of the war in Europe. On 19 March 1945, Fw 190D-9s of IV./JG 26 clashed with Mustangs of the 78th FG that were carrying out strafing attacks on the Luftwaffe's airfields in the Osnabrück area with the aim of preventing German fighters from rising to engage a force of more than 1,200 USAAF heavy bombers attacking targets in the central and southern Reich. Here, Leutnant Peter Crump describes how he claimed his 22nd victory (Caldwell, *Top Guns*, pg 366):

> I was returning from a mission around Münster – attempting to reach my home field at Varrelbusch at low altitude – when I spotted a Mustang. I followed the unsuspecting pilot and caught up to him near my airfield. When the Mustang came

within firing range, I surprised the pilot with a tight bank in the opposite direction. Unnerved, he immediately tried to take flight, and I was able to shoot him down without much resistance. He bailed out successfully, with moderate burns to his neck and head. At Varrelbusch that evening, I was able to congratulate him on his survival.

However, the experiences of 'Dora' pilot Feldwebel Gerhard Kroll of 15./JG 26 is more representative of the demise of many German fighter pilots at this stage of the war. The Fw 190D-9s of IV./JG 26 had been 'bombed out' of their base at Varrelbusch on 24 March by B-17s of the USAAF's 3rd BD, and so from 0600 hrs on the morning of the 25th, they began to transfer the short distance to the neighbouring airfield at Bissel, which had seen very little use until December 1944. Facilities there were rudimentary, consisting of wooden huts and some earth bunkers, but the dispersals were, fortunately and necessarily, wooden revetments concealed in beech woods on the airfield boundary, safely camouflaged from marauding Allied fighters and fighter-bombers. The IV. *Gruppe* machines joined a number of D-9s from II./JG 26 that had also flown into Bissel from Nordhorn that morning. Their base, too, had suffered from the American bombing of the previous day.

When they arrived, the pilots of IV. *Gruppe* were instructed to remain at readiness. In the late afternoon of 26 March, 15 D-9s from 13. and 15./JG 26 were ordered into the air to carry out a *freie Jagd* to the southwest as far as a line to the area along the Rhine between Rees and Kirchellen. Within the German fighter formation, Feldwebel Gerhard Kroll was assigned to fly as wingman to the *Staffelführer* of 15. *Staffel*, Oberleutnant Wilhelm Heilmann. It was not long before the 'Doras' encountered a formation of what were apparently Tempest Vs but the identity of which has never been confirmed. These aircraft had been reported to be on their way home after having carried out an offensive patrol and some ground-strafing. Kroll subsequently recalled:

> I was full of unrest all day. I knew if I had to go up, something would happen. All day long we were on the alert, on and off, on and off. That pulls at one's nerves. Finally, we had to go up to chase a group of Tempests.

The Focke-Wulfs climbed up to combat altitude in a wide spiral, but in doing so they did not cover much ground:

> This time I was flying as wingman to Oberleutnant Willi Heilmann, who was leading our squadron. The 13. *Staffel* always led the formation because Leutnant Crump had the best eyes. He could recognise the type and number of aircraft when the rest of us couldn't even see specks on the canopy.
>
> Heilmann placed us a little to the left side of our formation, so we were like in a 'spotter' position. But as the *Gruppe* began to turn and head to the right, and we continued veering to the left by double opposing movement, all of a sudden we found ourselves alone. I had no idea what Heilmann had in mind. I also have no idea what the rest of the *Gruppe* did after we split away.

Finally, at the Dutch border, we climbed, circled and made contact with the enemy. Circling and climbing to the right, we were pursued from below by three, possibly four, RAF Tempests. We could see they were better [in a climb] than our D-9s, and would soon reach us and overtake us. Suddenly, Heilmann changed from a right turn into a left turn and went into a steep dive. As far as I know, he didn't fire a shot. He just went – and for sure, I didn't fire a shot either.

That same second I knew I'd had it. If I stayed up I would have to fight it out with the three Tempests. If I followed Heilmann, I would cross in front of the guns of the first Tempest. All he had to do was press the buttons. And he did. Boy, did that rattle right and left and fore and aft! In the same instant my aircraft caught fire. So, in reality, this had been no dogfight, but rather a stupid manoeuvre which had *me* nailed.

Altitude was about 23,000ft. My aircraft went into a steep dive. I wanted to bail out but the canopy was jammed. Something up in front of me exploded and I received a face full of instruments. For a second I thought that was it, but my face hurt and I realised that I was still alive.

EARLY AFTERNOON, 19 MARCH 1945

BETWEEN RHEINE AIRFIELD AND HASELÜNNE

1 Forty-six P-51s of the USAAF's 78th FG are heading west in small groups after an encounter with Bf 109K-4s of IV./JG 27 over the Rheine area. The Mustang pilots are wary, but elated, having claimed several of the Messerschmitts shot down for the loss of only one of their own.

2 Shortly after 1330 hrs, a formation of between 20–25 Fw 190D-9s from IV./JG 26, under the command of Oberleutnant Hans Dortenmann and based at Varrelbusch, are flying towards the southeast at 4,000m over a heavily-forested region about 15km southwest of Quakenbrück. They have been briefed to undertake a *freie Jagd* in the Münster-Rheine area.

3 The two opposing formations spot each other over Rheine airfield and a large-scale dogfight ensues, with pilots from both sides keeping their wary eyes on their fuel gauges.

4 Dortenmann leads his formation towards the rear of the Mustangs. The Luftwaffe pilots spot eight American fighters below them, climbing up to engage IV./JG 26 head on, with a further five P-51s above in clouds. Dortenmann immediately enters into a climb and then dives towards one of the fleeing Mustangs.

5 At 1336 hrs, accompanied – in line astern – by the three comrades in his *Schwarm*, Dortenmann attacks from above and behind at 3,500m, semi-inverted while in a steep left turn, opening fire from just 50–20m.

6 The outer right wing of the Mustang is seen to break away, and the American machine falls into a vertical dive in flames. Dortenmann's 29th victim is Maj Harry Lee Downing, commander of the 78th FG's 84th FS. According to 2Lt Thomas V. Thain, also of the 84th FS, 'The Fw 190 pilots were the most aggressive and probably the most experienced of the enemy fighters. I saw Maj Downing shoot down one Me 109. Later I heard him say over the R/T that he had shot down another aircraft. He called and said there was a lot of meat there. I then heard him say he was hit and was bailing out. His last words were, "So Long, Gang." I recognised this voice as his right away.' Downing is able to bail out of his spinning P-51, which crashed near Lotten, 3km south of Haselünne.

FOLLOWING PAGES

I prepared to bail out but I found the canopy jammed. Eventually, I managed to crank it open about a foot when the slipstream ripped it completely off and sucked me out (I had previously released my harness). Then I was left in mid-air, about 13,000ft above the ground, wondering if my parachute had burned away. I didn't dare pull the ripcord. If it was on fire, one puff and I would go down like a stone. So I let myself fall until the trees appeared really big, and only at the last second did I pull the cord. After the opening thud, I made only one swing and I was down. Since the 'chute took about 250ft to fully open, I figure I pulled the cord at about 500ft. This was the third time I had been burned – boy, did I swear!

I did not know the exact location of my 'landing', and was told only that it was north of Bocholt. I came down in a field, and shortly afterwards I started to use the First Aid kit I had with me to attend to my burnt face. The small mirror I had with me was shattered, but I had managed to bandage my head when some German soldiers arrived. They drove me in a Kübelwagen to what was something akin to a nunnery. By then it was dark, and I was pretty well 'gone'. All I remember is the fuss this nun made about my parachute. It was soaked with fuel and stinking. I had to leave it outside. I didn't receive any treatment, but a little later an ambulance came and took me to Haaksbergen [across the border in the Netherlands].

While Kroll's injuries meant that his war was over, the remainder of his *Gruppe* had, in fact, engaged RAF Spitfires in the Bocholt area, one of which was claimed to have been shot down. There were no losses, however.

By late April, even the veteran pilots were feeling the strain of relentless alerts and operations. Oberleutnant Dortenmann felt the flying was 'becoming more and more miserable. We can hardly get off the ground.' That was because of the constant presence of Allied fighters. The only consolation, Dortenmann admitted, lay in 'cigarettes and alcohol', which kept the pilots going.

One highly experienced Luftwaffe pilot to end his war flying the D-9 was Oberleutnant Oskar Romm, the *Gruppenkommandeur* of IV./JG 3. By late April 1945 his personal victory tally stood at 92, the last claimed on 21 March when he had shot down one of several Il-2s that had attacked his *Gruppe's* base at Prenzlau. A small number of Focke-Wulfs had managed to get airborne during the attack, and two more *Shturmoviks* were claimed by D-9 pilots Feldwebel Oskar Bösch and Leutnant Karl-Alfred Schulte for their 16th and 3rd claims, respectively. Romm continued to fly missions after this episode, but five weeks later he would meet his match over an area of the front where Soviet forces had just broken through, as he recounted (Price, *At War*, pg 132–133):

My last combat mission was on 24 April 1945, to the south of Stettin, when, with my wingman, I attacked a formation of Russian *Shturmovik* ground-attack aircraft. I selected full emergency power, and with our superior speed we went right through the Russian fighter escort without difficulty. I was just about to open fire on one of the Ilyushins when my cooling gills suddenly opened automatically and the oil and coolant temperature gauges showed that the engine was overheating.

Either my engine had been hit by enemy fire or it had suffered a failure. I broke off the action by rolling over onto my back and pulling away in a steep dive. The Russian fighters endeavouring to follow were soon left behind and abandoned the chase.

Romm nursed his 'Dora' to the southwest, back towards the German frontline, with sparks and exhaust smoke trailing behind the damaged, overheating engine. 'As the last of the lubricating oil burned away between the aluminium pistons and the steel cylinder block,' he recalled, 'the engine burst into flames.' Romm had made it back to German-held territory, but he was too low to bail out. A short while later the Jumo cut out and the Fw 190D-9 pancaked into the ground near Brüssow, 20km northwest of Prenzlau. He recalled how the aircraft:

> . . . proceeded to smear its pieces all over the landscape. However, the same rugged construction that had saved my life in earlier emergency landings proved itself once again.

Despite the D-9's rugged build, Romm suffered a fractured skull, facial lacerations, concussion and other minor injuries. Fortunately, his landing was observed by soldiers at a nearby divisional headquarters, and they radioed his position to the local Luftwaffe command. The soldiers then removed him from his aircraft and took the fighter pilot to their headquarters, where an army doctor did his best to tend to him. Some hours later Romm

Oberleutnant Oskar Romm was awarded the Knight's Cross on 29 February 1944 when his score stood at 76, and by war's end he was credited with 92 aerial victories. Claiming his final victories with the 'Dora' whilst serving as the *Gruppenkommandeur* of IV./JG 3, Romm was badly injured when he had to force-land his burning D-9 on 24 April 1945 following an engagement with Soviet Il-2s. (EN Archive)

was collected from the area of the crash by personnel of IV./JG 3, led by an officer of the *Stabskompanie*, and taken firstly to a Luftwaffe hospital at Wismar and then, four days later, to another hospital at Timmendorfer-Strand on the Baltic coast near Travemünde. His war was over.

As the territory still controlled by the Third Reich became compressed from both the east and the west, so those Luftwaffe fighter units still operating began to fly missions over both the 'Western' and 'Eastern' Fronts – or at least that was how the lines were still officially referred to. By late April, Germans were quipping that it would be possible to catch a tram from one front to the other. Nevertheless, the Fw 190D-9 pilots fought on, their missions now being just as much about ground-attack as they were aerial combat. To that end, the 'Doras' of JG 26 conducted strafing and bombing missions against enemy troop concentrations, vehicle columns and bridges, usually in formations of some 20 or so aircraft, but on an increasingly less frequent basis.

Oberleutnant Oskar Romm's Fw 190D-9 at Prenzlau in March 1945. The fighter, marked with the double chevrons of a IV. *Gruppe* staff flight aircraft, is connected to a generator starter cart in preparation for an 'Alarmstart' take-off. (EN Archive)

On 15 April, 14. *Fliegerdivision* reported 19 D-9s of II. *Gruppe* carrying out low-level attacks in the Rethen-Schwarmstedt area, during which ten Spitfires were encountered. Feldwebel Willi Niedermeyer of 5. *Staffel* and his D-9 were lost. Further large-scale armed reconnaissance and attacks were carried out on enemy movements in the Soltau-Uelzen-Salzwedel areas later that same day. On the 17th, transport columns around Lüneburg and the Soltau-Verden areas were attacked, while on the 19th, an early morning 'reconnaissance in force' to the Lüneburg Heath area would be flown at low level over enemy positions – something that was necessary because fog presented a problem to vision.

Leutnant Siegfried Sy joined the Luftwaffe from the Wehrmacht in 1943, having fought as a soldier in the Polish campaign. Upon completion of his pilot training, he was assigned to II./JG 26 in March 1944. On 24 April 1945, Sy, the interim *Staffelkapitän* of 6./JG 26, had already flown a morning reconnaissance mission, leading four 'Doras' of 7. *Staffel*. They had spotted a column of enemy vehicles travelling along the main road to the Heath.

'Yellow 6', an Fw 190D-9 of II./JG 6, speeds down a sodden grass runway laden with a solitary SC 250 250kg bomb attached to an ETC 504 centreline rack at the start of another ground-attack mission. (EN Archive)

Based on Sy's reports, Fw 190D-9s of 6. *Staffel* had been scrambled, the aircraft laden with bombs to attack the Allied motor transport. As the 6. *Staffel* aircraft made their attack, back on the ground, Sy's aircraft was loaded with a bomb and he too took off for a second mission to attack the column at the head of 11 bomb-carrying D-9s from 5. and 7./JG 26. The German fighters flew in a disciplined formation, skirting south of Hamburg, over Harburg and towards Lüneburg Heath, where they came across the column. Sy recalled (Caldwell, *Top Guns*, pg 385):

> There were so many targets that we didn't know where to begin. We made a shallow turn to the left, and could now take the entire road under fire. My bomb unfortunately missed its target by a few metres, not striking the road itself, where it was aimed, but rather the ditch beside it.

As the D-9s made their bombing runs, they drew enemy ground fire and light antiaircraft fire, which had not been previously observed. This forced the Luftwaffe pilots to make evasive manoeuvres:

> One truck after another burst into flames. We jinked to the left and to the right along the road. To the left, beside the ditch, was a twin-barrel anti-aircraft gun. Gently, I stepped on the rudder pedal and pressed the firing button. The gun ceased fire immediately. The other pilots were firing as well. Here and there an Fw 190D flew along gracefully, dipping its 'snout' to 'graze' again and again from the highway. Now, however, it was enough. I banked to the left; behind me, the others were still at work. I gave the recall order over the radio, and we ended the bloody business. Most of us had used up all our ammo.

By 28 April, the *Jagdwaffe* was in a state of systematic disbandment. That day, the *Kommodore* of JG 51, Major Heinz Lange, met with Oberstleutnant Karl-Gottfried Nordmann, the *Inspekteur der Jagdflieger Ost* and *Jafü Nord Ost*, to discuss the immediate future. JG 51 had taken part in the air defence of Berlin, but such was the adverse situation in respect to fuel, parts and dwindling numbers of serviceable aircraft that a decision was taken to disband, officially, the bulk of the *Geschwader*, including the *Stab*, I. II. and III. *Gruppen*. Lange remembers (Hermann, *Fw 190 'Long Nose'*, pg 158–159):

> I had only recently assumed command of *Jagdgeschwader 'Mölders'* and had flown back to East Prussia, where the I. and III. *Gruppe* and the *Stabsstaffel* were located. There, all my efforts to get these elements of the *Geschwader* back were in vain: the I. *Gruppe* was disbanded and elements were incorporated into the III. *Gruppe*, while all remaining personnel were supposed to go to the army.
>
> I nevertheless managed to get a large part of the membership of the *Geschwader* back to Swinemünde. From there, on 28 April, we proceeded to Schmoldow, in Pomerania, where we re-joined the IV. *Gruppe*, our air signals company and the elements of the *Stabsstaffel* that had remained there. At that airfield we took on

strength several Fw 190D-9s. This type was the best the Luftwaffe had to offer, apart from the Me 262.

This meant that Oberleutnant Günther Josten's IV./JG 51 was the only functioning *Gruppe* of the *Geschwader*. This unit, operating its small number of Fw 190D-9s, had within its ranks one Knight's Cross with Oak Leaves recipient in the form of Oberleutnant Josten (who, having served with JG 51 since 1942, had completed 420 missions and been credited with 178 victories) and no fewer than six other holders of the Knight's Cross, including Major Lange and 22-year-old Oberfeldwebel Heinz Marquardt of 13./JG 51, who had flown 320 missions. Lange recalled:

> The D-9 was somewhat longer because of its Jumo 213 engine and the annular radiator in front of it. It was somewhat inferior to other versions of the Fw 190 in a turn, but it had an outstanding rate of climb. It also had an excellent turn of speed in level flight. There was no opportunity to test-fly the aircraft, for we had to move again the next day, to Neu Lübke. Over Neubrandenburg, we encountered four Soviet La-7s. In the ensuing engagement, Oberfeldwebel [Alfred] Rauch, formerly of the *Stabsstaffel* [and a veteran of 681 sorties with JG 51] who had recently been awarded the Knight's Cross [he had received it the previous day], shot down one of the enemy aircraft for the unit's last victory [and his 59th].

Major Heinz Lange, the last *Kommodore* of JG 51, felt that the Fw 190D-9 was 'the best the Luftwaffe had to offer, apart from the Me 262'. In June 1945 Lange, a 73-victory Knight's Cross-holder, also took part in a mock dogfight between an Fw 190D-13 (a revised D sub-variant built with an MG 151/20E engine-mounted cannon and two similar weapons in the wing roots) and a Tempest V. The Allied observers of this unique engagement were very impressed by the performance of the Focke-Wulf, and they duly requested that surviving examples be sent to Britain and the USA for further inspection. (EN Archive)

With this victory, IV. *Gruppe* had shot down 115 enemy aircraft against just five losses in the final three weeks of the war, or since the start of the Battle of Berlin. On 30 April we moved to Redlin, near Parchim. On 1 May we flew a mission over Schwerin and Berlin. Oberfeldwebel Marquardt and Oberfeldwebel Buss were lost in this engagement – this time our opponents were Spitfires.

That same day (1 May), British forces under Field Marshal Montgomery continued their drive across northern Germany and advanced from the Elbe towards Berlin virtually unopposed. Adolf Hitler had just committed suicide in Berlin, where there was now street-fighting with the Soviet Red Army, and Reichsmarschall Hermann Göring was under house arrest in southern Germany for attempting to seize control of what remained of the Third Reich as a result of the *Führer's* self-imposed incarceration. In the air, the *Jagdwaffe* continued its last, spasmodic but defiant defensive operations on both the Western and Eastern Fronts.

During the late morning on the 1st, a formation of six Fw 190D-9s from IV./JG 51 under the command of Oberfeldwebel Heinz Marquardt took off from Redlin to escort a formation of ground-attack aircraft to Berlin, after which they were to conduct a *freie Jagd*.

In an operational career flying the Bf 109 and Fw 190, Heinz Marquardt, who had joined JG 51 in August 1943, was accredited with 121 victories (with 16 more unconfirmed), all scored on the Eastern Front, with IV./JG 51 (initially 15. *Staffel*, then 13. *Staffel*). His tally included 77 Soviet fighters, 24 twin-engined medium bombers and 20 Il-2s, and on 7 October 1944, he downed eight enemy aircraft in one day. Marquardt was awarded the Knight's Cross on 18 November 1944. He was himself shot down seven times. Between February and August 1942 Marquardt had served as an instructor pilot in southern France, where he earned the nickname 'Negus' on account of the deep suntan he acquired while there.

Prior to the clash on 1 May, Marquardt had already proved potent at the controls of the D-9 after being credited with shooting down four Yak-3s while ferrying a 'Dora' to Prenzlau on 24 April.

Once they had concluded their mission on 1 May, the Fw 190D-9s returned with the fighter-bombers to Schwerin after what was intended to have been the unit's last operation before surrendering to Allied forces.

The unfortunate demise of Fw 190D-9 'White 13' of 13./JG 51 photographed at Klein-Lübke, a landing ground south of Rostock, on 30 April 1945 following Leutnant Kurt Tanzer's accidental manoeuvring of the aircraft into a ditch, which has left the VS 9 propeller splintered. At right, Oberfeldwebel Heinz Marquardt observes the scene. (John Weal Collection)

Fahnenjunker-Oberfeldwebel Heinz Marquardt of IV./JG 51 poses for the camera wearing the Knight's Cross awarded to him on 18 November 1944. One of the leading Fw 190D-9 aces, he accounted for 21 enemy aircraft in the two weeks between 14 April and 1 May 1945. Marquardt ended the war with 121 victories to his name. (EN Archive)

Flt Lt Peter Cowell of No 41 Sqn destroyed two Fw 190D-9s whilst at the controls of a Spitfire XIV over Lake Schwerin on 1 May 1945. One of his victims was Fahnenjunker-Oberfeldwebel Heinz Marquardt of IV./JG 51. (Andrew Thomas Collection)

At 1300 hrs, as they commenced their approach to the airfield, the formation was spotted by six Spitfire XIVs from No 41 Sqn that had been detailed to conduct a sweep around Lake Schwerin and the neighbouring airfield.

Two of the Spitfire pilots, Flt Lt Peter Cowell and Flg Off Walter Jallands, climbed to 6,000ft and then turned back over Lake Schwerin, whereupon they observed 'two long-nosed Fw 190s flying east at zero feet over the water'. These were flown by Marquardt and his wingman, Feldwebel Heinz 'Piefke' Radlauer, of 13./JG 51. Radlauer had been flying the D-9 regularly since 20 April from Prenzlau, Schmoldow and Neu Lübke, and his sorties had included a *Jabo* mission to Berlin and a *freie Jagd*.

Cowell and Jallands dived and chased the D-9s across the lake, with Cowell opening fire at 300 yards on the right-hand Focke-Wulf. The German fighters, by this point separated from the rest of their formation, broke away in opposite directions, Marquardt turning sharply to the right while Radlauer banked left. With Cowell closing in to 50 yards, his guns registered hits on Marquardt's aircraft. The Focke-Wulf climbed almost vertically, streaming black smoke, then flipped over as pieces flew off it. Moments later it crashed close to the southeastern shore of the lake.

Cowell then attacked a third D-9 that he had spotted orbiting to the north. Again, he closed in to 50 yards. 'A large piece flew off his port wing', Cowell reported subsequently, 'and the pilot bailed out, the aircraft crashing near the first one.'

Injured by a hard blow to the back of the head from debris caused by the Spitfire's cannon shells, Marquardt had fallen forward and hit his nose on the gunsight. He managed to bail out, however, and landed in the grounds of a nearby hospital, where he was found half-conscious hanging from his parachute outside a window of a nurses' home. The canopy had become snared on one of the chimneys. The nurses were able to haul him in through the window and, as Heinz Radlauer later recalled, 'That was the end of his war!'

Feldwebel Radlauer escaped at tree-top height towards Flensburg pursued by another Spitfire. However, Radlauer, an experienced 100-mission Eastern Front *jagdflieger* with 15 victories, including four *Shturmoviks* and two Yak-3s shot down in one mission two weeks earlier, was able to outrun his assailant and land at Flensburg.

Commenting on this engagement, the war diary of IV./JG 51 recorded:

Against destiny we are all helpless. This was shown on 1 May when our Oberfeldwebel Marquardt – honoured and recognised by the *Gruppe* as being one of our finest fighter pilots – was shot down by a Spitfire over Schwerin during the very last mission of the war.

Rare Fw 190D-13 Wk-Nr. 836017 'Yellow 10', formerly of *Stab* JG 26 at Gilze-Rijen, was evaluated at Flensburg in June 1945. Here, having had USAAF markings applied (a white star can just be seen on the underside of each wing), it was flown at least twice by veteran aces from JG 51 in mock combat against a Tempest V. Note the fighter's large paddle-bladed VS 9 propeller and lack of provision for outboard wing guns. (EN Archive)

JG 51's *Kommodore*, Heinz Lange, recalled, 'We never heard any more of Oberfeldwebel Buss'. The latter was almost certainly at the controls of the second Fw 190D-9 claimed by Cowell.

In summing up the Fw 190D-9, Lange commented, 'I will never forget that we found the machine fantastic'.

EARLY AFTERNOON, 1 MAY 1945

LAKE SCHWERIN, NORTHERN GERMANY

1 At 1300 hrs, six Spitfire XIVs of No 41 Sqn's Red Section are on patrol just east of Lake Schwerin. The fighters are led by Flt Lt Peter Cowell.

2 They spot, and bounce, enemy aircraft observed near Schwerin-Görries airfield, on the western shore of the lake. Red 3 and 4 break away to attack, and Red 5 and 6 chase another fighter.

3 Red 1 (Cowell) and Red 2 (Flg Off Walter Jallands) descend towards the lake.

4 Red 1 and Red 2 then turn back east and climb towards cumulous cloud at 1,800m. They then spot two Fw 190D-9s, flown by Oberfeldwebel Heinz Marquardt and Feldwebel Heinz Radlauer, flying at 'zero feet' over the lake. Both 'Dora' pilots, from 15./JG 51, commence their low-level approach to Schwerin-Görries airfield, having returned from an escort mission for ground attack aircraft.

5 Cowell and Jallands close in on Marquardt and Radlauer. Cowell opens fire at Marquardt's Focke-Wulf from a distance of 275m. The 'Dora' pilots split to evade their pursuers. Marquardt climbs almost vertically up to the right, while Radlauer veers off to the left.

6 Cowell closes to 45m, continuing to fire. The D-9 flicks over onto its back and Marquardt falls out of the cockpit and lands in the grounds of a nearby hospital, where he is found half-conscious hanging from his parachute outside a window of a nurses' home. The pilotless 'Dora' crashes near the southeastern shore of the lake.

FOLLOWING PAGES

AFTERMATH

The Focke-Wulf Fw 190D-9 was one of the few fighter designs to see service in World War 2 that had been designed after the outbreak of hostilities.

Following the D-9, there was some limited development of ensuing variants, but things got off to a bad start with the D-10 which was designed to conform to a requirement from the RLM that all fighters be capable of carrying a centrally-mounted, larger-calibre weapon. Focke-Wulf thus proposed mounting a 20mm cannon asymmetrically in the forward fuselage.

The Fw 190D-11 was intended for ground-attack operations, and was to be powered by the Jumo 213F, in which the supercharger was cooled by MW (50/50 Methanol Water) injection and armed with two wing-mounted MG 151/20E and two similarly mounted MK 108 cannon, although the fitment of underwing 21cm mortars was deleted.

The existing Fw 190 prototypes V57 to V61 were assigned for conversion to D-11 configuration, and they were used primarily for engine testing. Production commenced in January 1945, but this was stymied by lack of availability of the Jumo engine, which meant that the DB 603 was proposed as a replacement. The limited numbers of aircraft that did appear from 1944 were delivered to the *Verbandführerschule* of the *General der Jagdflieger*, the *Stab* and II./JG 300 and JV 44. In January it was proposed to equip the Jumo 213F-powered D-12 variant with a two-stage, three-speed supercharger and arm it with an 85-round 30mm MK 108 cannon intended for firing centrally through the propeller hub. This weapon would augment two wing root-mounted 20mm MG 151/20Es with 220 rounds per gun. Three prototypes, the V62–V64, were assigned for D-12 testing at Dessau and Tarnewitz between November 1944 and February 1945, but this was very limited, and it is questionable as to what extent, if any, the V64 actually took part in the process. The Jumo 213F also proved problematic.

Two more prototypes, the V65 and V71, were slated as experimental D-13 test machines to carry a centrally-mounted MG 151/20E. It was hoped to commence D-12 production in February 1945 and D-13 production in January, but this did not happen.

Despite the Fw 190D-9 being a superlative all-round fighter, by mid-1944 the sun was beginning to set on the era of piston-engined interceptors as jet engine technology evolved and progressed. Nevertheless, in 1944, as concerns grew about the possible appearance of the B-29 over Europe, Kurt Tank began to develop another fighter that would emerge as the Ta 152. Inspired by the D-9, this high-altitude interceptor, with a longer fuselage than the 'Dora', did arrive with the Luftwaffe in limited numbers from January 1945. The greater wingspan of the Jumo 213-engined Ta 152 meant that it could reach high-altitude quickly and fly at height more efficiently than its shorter-winged predecessor. But the B-29 never came to Europe.

SELECTED SOURCES

Caldwell, Donald, *JG 26 – Top Guns of the Luftwaffe: The Epic Saga of Germany's Greatest Fighter Wing* (Orion Books, New York, 1991)

Caldwell, Donald, *The JG 26 War Diary – Volume Two 1943–1945* (Grub Street, London, 1998)

Crandall, Jerry, *The Focke-Wulf Fw 190 Dora – Volume One Fw 190D-9* (Eagle Editions, Hamilton, 2007)

Crandall, Jerry, *The Focke-Wulf Fw 190 Dora – Volume Two Fw 190D-9, D-11, D-13* (Eagle Editions, Hamilton, 2009)

Deboeck, Marc, Larger, Eric and Poruba, Tomás, *Focke-Wulf Fw 190D – Camouflage & Markings Part I* (JaPo, Hradec-Králové, 2005)

Deboeck, Marc, Larger, Eric and Poruba, Tomás, *Focke-Wulf Fw 190D – Camouflage & Markings Part II* (JaPo, Hradec-Králové, 2007)

Eriksson, Patrick G., *Alarmstart South and Final Defeat – The German Fighter Pilot's Experience in the Mediterranean Theatre 1941–44 and Normandy, Norway and Germany 1944–45* (Amberley Publishing, Stroud, 2019)

Hermann, Dietmar, *Focke-Wulf Fw 190 'Long Nose' – An Illustrated History of the Fw 190D Series* (Schiffer Publishing, Atglen, 2003)

Manrho, John and Pütz, Ron, *Bodenplatte: The Luftwaffe's Last Hope – The Attack on Allied Airfields, New Year's Day 1945* (Hikoki Publications, Crowborough, 2004)

Prien, Jochen, *IV./Jagdgeschwader 3 – Chronik einer Jagdgruppe 1943–1945* (Struve-Druck, Eutin, undated)

Priller, Josef, *J.G.26 – Geschichte eines Jagdgeschwaders: Das J.G.26 (Schlageter) 1937–1945* (Motorbuch Verlag, Stuttgart, 1980)

Rodeike, Peter, *Focke-Wulf Jagdflugzeug – Fw 190A, Fw 190 'Dora', Ta 152H* (Struve-Druck, Eutin, no date)

Smith, J. Richard, and Creek, Eddie J., *Focke-Wulf Fw 190 Volume Three 1944–1945* (Classic Publications, Hersham, 2013)

Urbanke, Axel, *Green Hearts – First in Combat with the Dora 9* (Eagle Editions, Hamilton, 1998)

Jakl, Christian, 'Oblt Hans Dortenmann – Flying Ace: His Aircraft and their History' at www.rlm.at/cont/gal23_e.htm

Kitchens III, Dr. James H., and Kroll, Gerhard H., *Luftwaffe service career* (private document, 1990)

Kroll, Gerhard, various correspondence with author 1991–93

WWII Aircraft Performance at www.wwiiaircraftperformance.org: FW 190 D-9 Flight Trials

INDEX